Raising Lombardi

What It Takes to Claim
Football's Ultimate Prize

Ross Bernstein

Forewords by Michael Strahan
& Daryl "Moose" Johnston

TRIUMPH
BOOKS

Library of Congress Cataloging-in-Publication Data

Bernstein, Ross.
    Raising Lombardi : what it takes to claim football's ultimate prize / Ross Bernstein ; forewords by Michael Strahan & Daryl "Moose" Johnston.
        p. cm.
    ISBN 978-1-60078-616-7
        1. Football. 2. Super Bowl. I. Title.

GV951.B355 2011
796.332'648—dc23

                                        2011025592

This book is available in quantity at special discounts for your group or organization. For further information, contact:

Triumph Books
542 South Dearborn Street
Suite 750
Chicago, Illinois 60605
(312) 939-3330
Fax (312) 663-3557
www.triumphbooks.com

Printed in U.S.A.
ISBN: 978-1-60078-616-7
Design by Amy Carter

For Sara and Campbell

Contents

Foreword
Michael Strahan

You play the game to win championships; that's what it's all about. You just hope that you can play the game the right way, and for the right reasons, play long enough, and in the end get an opportunity to win that beautiful trophy. I was fortunate to be a member of the Giants in 2008, right at the end of my career, and what else can you say? It was an amazing experience. To raise it, for me, was just the accumulation of all the years, all the hard work, and all the teammates that I had played with and learned from. All of that goes through your mind as you are raising the Lombardi Trophy. It's like an out-of-body experience as it all sort of flashes before your eyes. It was surreal. In fact, it's still surreal when I go back and watch the tape again all these years later. It's just something that they can never take away from you. Ever.

The 2007–08 Giants were a team of destiny. What an amazing group of guys, and what a privilege to be a member of that team. From Coach Coughlin all the way on down, what a team that was. There were a lot of factors in why that team won. For starters, we were focused and were dedicated to one another. We worked really hard and held each other accountable. I also think we enjoyed being the underdog. I really do. We liked playing on the road. That brought us together and made us stronger. We enjoyed it when people didn't give us a chance to win. We relished that role and took it personally when they tried to disrespect us. Look, I had been on other teams in New York that were full of talented players, but nothing was like this team. Nothing. It was special. It was a team of destiny.

I think the defining moment for us that year was when we lost to New England in the last game of the regular season. New England was such a good team, undefeated up until that point, and we hung in there with them. It was a close game, and that gave us a lot of confidence. We didn't really go all out to prepare for it either, because we knew that we were going to make the playoffs regardless. We didn't want to give away our game plan to Tampa Bay, who we were playing the following week in the first round of the playoffs, so we were pretty vanilla in everything we did. We just felt that if we could get that close and play that well against those guys despite not showing them our game plan then we knew we would have a chance if we played them again later in the postseason. From there, we just got on a roll, and I guess the rest is history—truly a storybook ending—right up until the way it all ended.

We came in as a wild card, and nobody was expecting us to make much noise. After we beat Tampa Bay, we headed to top-seeded Dallas. They had beaten us twice in the regular season, and we were anxious for some payback. Eli Manning hooked up with Amani Toomer for a couple of touchdowns early, and we went into the half tied at 14–14. Brandon Jacobs scored late for us, and from there we just held them off right up until the last second. I will never forget when R.W. McQuarters intercepted Cowboys quarterback Tony Romo in the end zone as time expired. We won 21–17, and with that we were going to the NFC Championship Game.

Next up were the Green Bay Packers, up at Lambeau in what would turn out to be one of the coldest games in NFL history—something like -25°F wind chill. It was so cold out there, just unbelievable. We jumped out to an early lead in this one on

Michael Strahan holds up the Vince Lombardi Trophy as he rides in New York's victory parade on February 5, 2008, following the Giants' victory in Super Bowl XLVII. (AP Images)

a pair of field goals, only to see Brett Favre hit Donald Driver on a 90-yard touchdown pass in the second quarter to take a 7–6 lead. They then went up 10–6 at the half. We answered in the third on Brandon Jacobs' touchdown, and they answered right back when Favre hit Donald Lee on a short touchdown to make it 17–13. We took the lead yet again when Ahmad Bradshaw ran one in, but they tied it on a field goal to send it to overtime. They were driving late, and it was looking bleak, when Corey Webster intercepted Favre and gave us the ball back. We then drove down and won it on Lawrence Tyne's game-winning 47-yard field goal. We were going to the Super Bowl. Wow, what a feeling that was!

From there we headed to Phoenix, where we now had the monumental task of beating the 18–0 undefeated New England Patriots, who everybody thought would just kill us. Boy were they wrong! As a defense, we knew we were good. We led the league in sacks that season, and we were ready for them. They were 12-point favorites going in, and we thought that was great. That was just where we wanted to be, underdogs, disrespected. This one would turn out to be a classic. We went up 3–0 early, and then they came right back to make it 7–3 on a Lawrence Maroney touchdown. It was a defensive battle from there, but we hung in there. We were still down 7–3 into the fourth quarter but then took the lead when Eli hit David Tyree on a short touchdown pass. It was huge because that was Tyree's first TD all year. Tom Brady brought the Patriots back, though, and when he connected with Randy Moss late in the game, we were getting nervous. So it all came down to a final drive. The whole season came down to Eli scrambling around in the final moments of the game and hitting Tyree on a spectacular 32-yard catch that he sort of pinned to his helmet with one hand. Nobody could believe he held on to it. It was one of the greatest plays I've ever seen. That kept us alive, and then with just about a half minute to go in the game, Eli hit Plaxico Burress for what would turn out to be the game-winner.

We all went nuts, we couldn't believe it. We had done it. Our epic ride through the playoffs was complete. We were truly the road warriors that year. I mean, when it was all said and done, we rattled off 11 consecutive road wins, so going on the road for the postseason was no big deal to us. Celebrating out on the field after that, I will never forget it, it was just unbelievable. To get to play in the Super Bowl was something I will never forget. There were so many great memories, but aside from the sack and tipped ball and hitting Tom Brady, the one thing that stands out in my mind the most is standing on the podium after the game holding the Lombardi Trophy. Just standing there, watching the confetti rain down on my teammates and coaches as they were all smiling and hugging one another, that was my moment. To see the pure joy and happiness in their eyes was something I will never forget. It was a surprised look of "Wow! we really did this, even though nobody thought we could." I just thought about how hard we had all worked and about what we had all gone through together up until that point. I was so proud. Proud to be a Giant and proud of my teammates. It was incredible. That was when it really hit me: I was a champion. That moment was *it* for me; it was way better than any one play in the game. That was *my* moment, and it was so sweet.

When it was over, I really thought about retiring right then and there, like Jerome Bettis had done a few years earlier with Pittsburgh. But I wanted to make sure it was all out of my system before I hung 'em up for good. I didn't want to make a dramatic retirement speech out on the field, only to have to make a comeback a few months later. I waited a couple of months and really thought about whether or not I was ready to let it all go. I needed to know in my head if I was done playing this great game. In the end I was. I was ready. Football will always be in my blood, but I was ready to tackle the next phase of life as a broadcaster and analyst. It was a great career, and I wanted to go out on top, which I was fortunate enough to do. So no regrets. None.

Winning the Super Bowl taught me so much about life. It taught me perseverance. If you believe in something enough and you work hard enough at it, then you can make it happen. Anything is possible. In a game like football, though, you can't do it alone. You *have* to have great people around you. You have to surround yourself with great teammates who make you better. That teaches you humility. You learn pretty quickly that you aren't always going to be that star every week. You need your teammates to step up around you when you aren't having your best game. You learn about roles and about how everybody has to do his job, collectively, for the team to be successful. You need to have a great team around you, that was my big takeaway, and it's the same in business too—you have to surround yourself with good people whom you can trust. Once you have that, the sky is the limit.

—Michael Strahan, Defensive End
New York Giants, Super Bowl XLVII Champion

Foreword

Daryl "Moose" Johnston

Winning the Super Bowl, it's the realization of a childhood dream. I grew up watching football on Sundays with my father and brother, and we couldn't wait to watch the Super Bowl. So to find yourself one day not only playing in that game, but winning it, it's almost beyond words. It's surreal. Winning it, that's the culmination of years and years of hard work and sacrifice, and it all kind of comes together in a very short amount of time. When you win it for the first time, it's actually pretty overwhelming. You have all these different emotions that you're going through as the game ends, and you're not really sure what to do.

Winning three titles in four years was pretty amazing. Each team had its own story, though, its own journey. The '92 Super Bowl team was unique in that it probably had the least amount of adversity. A lot of people felt like we were still a few years away from being a legitimate contender at that point and that San Francisco was still the team to beat. We beat Buffalo in Pasadena that year 52–17 to win it, but I will still contend that the NFC Championship Game where we beat the Niners was probably the best game that group ever played over the entire four-year run.

The '93 season got off to a rough start because our star running back, Emmitt Smith, held out with a contract dispute. We lost our first two games, and then right away we started hearing all the talk that no team had ever started out 0–2 and gone on to win the Super Bowl. That would prove to be a good motivation for us. Well, Emmitt finally came back, and we picked up right where we left off. We finished the season with just two more losses and had a lot of confidence going into the playoffs. We first beat Green Bay and then got past San Francisco in the NFC Championship Game, which set up another rematch with Buffalo in the Super Bowl. The Bills were ready for us this time and gave us everything they had. They shut down Emmitt in the first half, and we were down 13–6 at halftime. I remember Jimmy Johnson telling us in the locker room that in order to neutralize them, we were going to be running a play that we hadn't run in about six weeks. I thought that our staff did their best job ever with halftime adjustments because we came out and really took it to them. It was Emmitt left and then Emmitt right on that same play every time as we drove down the field and scored. The momentum shifted from there, and we rolled, 30–13, to make it back-to-back Super Bowls.

This was Buffalo's fourth straight Super Bowl loss, and just seeing the looks on those guys' faces after the game, that was tough. I grew up just outside of Buffalo in upstate New York as a Bills fan, so it was definitely mixed emotions for me. I knew what that team meant to that community and knew how badly those fans wanted a championship. I don't think they have ever really gotten the proper credit that they deserve for going to four straight Super Bowls. They had a very dynamic team in those days, and even though I was out there celebrating with my teammates, I truly felt for those guys.

As for the '95 season, we had gotten beat by San Francisco in the '94 NFC Championship Game, so we were hungry to reclaim what we felt was ours. This was an interesting season. We had a lot of adversity that challenged us throughout the year. We were getting older, for starters, and we had also lost a

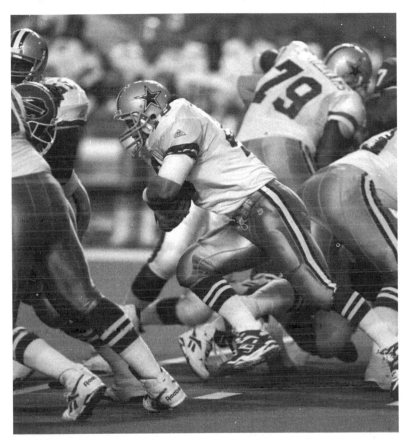

Daryl Johnston carries the ball during the Dallas Cowboys' 30–13 Super Bowl XXVIII victory over the Buffalo Bills in 1994. Johnston's Cowboys teams won three Super Bowls in the 1990s. (AP Images)

little bit of our toughness. One of the big reasons for that was due to the fact that our tough guy, Erik Williams, had missed most of the '94 season after being in a car accident. He came back in '95, but he was never the same player that he was prior to being injured. Overall, we just weren't the same team that we were three years ago. We played up and down all year and actually took a nose dive in December, losing some key divisional games and really just playing awful.

The playoffs came, and to be honest, we were just hoping for the best. Now, at that time there was sort of a dynamic going on: Green Bay was struggling against us, we were struggling against San Francisco, and San Francisco was struggling against Green Bay. Well, as luck would have it, Green Bay beat San Francisco on the road in the divisional round, and as a result we wound up with home-field advantage. And, more importantly, we got Green Bay versus San Francisco, who had our number. The Packers came to Dallas and gave us everything they had, but we hung in there and won the game, 38–27. I remember scoring on a 99-yard drive right before halftime in that one, and that really set the tone. From there we headed down to Phoenix to play Pittsburgh in Super Bowl XXX. We had control of this one from the get-go. The big momentum swinger for us was the Michael Irvin touchdown pass that was negated for offensive pass interference. We certainly did not agree with the call, but either way that play kind of rallied us together and gave us a boost of adrenaline. They came after us in the second half and made some great adjustments. When they got that onside kick and went down and closed that gap, we were all really nervous. Larry Brown had two big interceptions and was the hero for us in this one. Hey, sometimes it's better to be lucky than good. Emmitt had a couple of touchdowns, and Troy Aikman played great and didn't have any turnovers. The Steelers had a great football team that year, but we just kept after it and wound up winning the game, 27–17.

Three Super Bowls, three very different stories. What was special about all those teams was the fact that we were all very close. The relationships that we had with one another, including the coaches, went beyond being teammates. We were friends. We would go out in big groups, players as well as coaches, on Thursday nights and have dinner and then go bowling. Stuff like that was so much fun. We enjoyed each other's company; it wasn't just a job for us, we genuinely liked each other. It was like a second family. You oftentimes hear coaches talk about that, but I think Jimmy Johnson did a really good job, along with his staff, of creating that environment for us. We had a lot of high-profile players in those days, and whenever there was an issue or a problem with somebody, you would see a lot of the guys stand in support of that person. We did have quite a bit of controversy and adversity through our run, but everybody had a united front. Nobody would speak against anybody in the family; it was like you were protecting your brother. It was unique, that circle-the-wagon mentality, where we were all inside, and nobody else could get in unless we let them in. We just had a great foundation based on friendship, and that was the source of our success, I think.

None of this would have been possible without great leadership, and that started at the top with our coach, Jimmy Johnson. Jimmy had that unique ability where as a player you wanted to earn his respect. He was very smart and worked extremely hard. He challenged you on a daily basis and ran a tight ship. He was a big disciplinarian and kept us on a short leash, yet he wanted us to enjoy ourselves when we did have success. It was just all about success and excellence with him. We had a real family environment in the locker room under Jimmy; he really cared about his players. He generated a lot of confidence with our group. He saw early on that we had the makings of something special, too. I mean, he had a vision even back when we were really struggling—remember, we were 1–15 in '89—and he believed in us. When he saw how good Troy Aikman, Emmitt Smith, and Michael Irvin were going to be, he started game planning around those guys. The "triplets," as they were known, they were the key. He had a plan, a vision, and the fruits of that plan would result in three Super Bowls. So, you have to take your hat off to the guy: he's just an outstanding coach. There are very few people whom I have played for in my life who can generate an environment where you want to perform well to earn the respect of that person. Jimmy had that quality.

There were a lot of life lessons that I took away from those games, but the big one is that you can never stop learning and growing. I had so many great coaches along the way, from high school to college to the NFL to even now as a broadcaster. I've been fortunate to have been around some great people during my career. As a player, I wanted to learn as much as I possibly could so I could be the best I could be and help my teammates to win ballgames. Now, as a broadcaster, I have that same passion. Luckily I've been blessed to have been able to work with some amazing journalists along the way. I started out working with Bill Macatee, who was fantastic. I worked with Kevin Harlan, and then Dick Stockton, and now Kenny Albert. These are amazingly talented professionals who are among the very best at what they do. The fact that they have been kind enough to serve as mentors to me is extremely humbling. The biggest thing I've learned from all of them is to just listen. I was taught as a kid to "listen to understand before you speak to be understood," and I still think that rings true. You can learn a lot if you just listen to what people are trying to tell you.

Beyond that, part of learning and growing is being prepared, and preparation has always been a big thing for me. I've never felt like I was the most talented, I've never felt I was the smartest, I've never felt I was the most gifted, but I will outwork you. That is the one thing that I can control, the amount of effort that I put into something. You may be smarter than me, and you may be more physically gifted than me, but you're never going to outwork me. A lot of my battles were already won before I ever walked onto the field, because all of that preparation and hard work gave me confidence. From there it was just going out and executing the game plan.

Being humble was pretty big for me, too. I think you have to be a little bit humble and selfless in order to have success. It's all about the team when you get to this level, not about the individuals. Hey, I blocked for the all-time leading rusher in NFL history. I made holes for a living, and he got all the glory. That was my role, and I was proud to do it. Whenever he scored a touchdown, I felt like I was a big part of that right alongside of him. We all had roles, and some of them were not very glamorous, but we all had to do them to the best of our abilities for the good of the team. That was what it was all about. Not only did everybody on those teams accept their roles, they excelled at them. Whether it was me blocking for Emmitt or Bill Bates sacrificing his body on special teams, we all just did what we had to do. There was nobody more humble on our team than Troy Aikman. He accepted the fact that we were a run-first team and embraced it. He was not motivated by statistics. If Emmitt ran for four touchdowns and he didn't complete any passes, he didn't care. He just wanted to win, that was it. He was selfless in that regard, and that was why the guys respected him so much. So being humble was a big thing for me. I may not talk about it very much, but I take a lot of pride in that.

The other big takeaway for me was the ability to work together with different people, from across all racial and religious lines. Tolerance, communication, trust—that was all a part of it. To be in a locker room or in a huddle with so many diverse individuals from so many different backgrounds, and to see that group come together through a common goal, that's amazing. So to be a part of that really inspired me to be the best I could be. To be able to put everything else aside and get along with everybody and come together, what an incredible thing. I think that's why professional athletes are so coveted in business, because companies know that if you can work with absolutely anybody, and under extreme conditions of stress and pressure, then that's an extremely valuable skill set. It can be a tough transition though, no question. I mean, as an athlete, we saw things in black and white. You win, you lose. You're a starter, you're a backup. You're on the team, you're cut. Then, when you get out into the real world, everything is in shades of grey. And you realize that it's not a performance-based society that we live in, which is the polar opposite of the professional sports world. The cultures are totally different. It's a struggle and transition, but if you keep learning and growing, you work hard and prepare, you can work with different people, and you stay humble—then the world is your oyster.

—Daryl "Moose" Johnston, Fullback, Dallas Cowboys
Super Bowl XXVII, XXVIII, and XXX Champion

Introduction

Welcome to *Raising Lombardi: What it Takes to Claim Football's Ultimate Prize.* As for the genesis of this book, it's the sequel to my 2010 best seller titled *Raising Stanley*, in which I interviewed more than 100 hockey players and coaches who all had one thing in common: their names were etched onto Lord Stanley's holy grail. While the history of the Stanley Cup goes all the way back to 1893, the Vince Lombardi Trophy has only been around since 1967. As such, of the roughly 100 players and coaches I interviewed for *Raising Lombardi*, some have won Super Bowls, while others have won NFL championships—which is what the players competed for prior to that.

Okay, quick history lesson: the National Football League inaugurated play in 1920 as the American Professional Football Association. It didn't change its name and become the NFL until 1922. From the beginning through 1932, "champions" were determined by their win-loss record—not by virtue of a championship game. That all changed in 1933, however, when a playoff system was incorporated, and the league's two division winners competed for the Ed Thorp Memorial Trophy at season's end. The rival AFL began play in 1960, meanwhile, and also used a playoff system to determine its champion. Immediately, the two leagues began to compete for players, respect, and bragging rights. In 1966, the NFL and AFL agreed to merge, with a championship game between the two leagues to be played at the end of that season. (It would ultimately be a four-year process of merging.) Lamar Hunt, owner of the AFL's Kansas City Chiefs, suggested to then–NFL commissioner Pete Rozelle that the game be called the "Super Bowl." Hunt would later say the name was likely in his head because his children had been playing with a Super Ball toy in his office, and it just "came to him." (Technically, the 1966 and 1967 title games were called the "AFL-NFL World Championship Game," as the title *Super Bowl* did not become official until 1968. Thus the third AFL-NFL matchup was dubbed "Super Bowl III," with the first two being "retro-named" as Super Bowls I and II.) The first two title games were won convincingly by the NFL's Green Bay Packers, while the AFL's New York Jets and Hunt's Chiefs won Nos. III and IV. With the leagues even at 2–2 in "World Championship" competition, the AFL-NFL merger finally became official in 1970 (featuring the National Football Conference versus the American Football Conference) and has been known ever since as the NFL. Got all that? Good.

As for my criteria about whom I interviewed for the book? In addition to being champions, first and foremost, I wanted to get a true sampling of opinions. So, there's a wonderful mix of superstars and role players who cover all the positions out on the gridiron. From quarterbacks to nose tackles to kickers, they're all in here—and from all eras, too. In fact, I was able to interview at least one player from nearly every team over the past half century—going all the way back to Frank Gifford, who won a championship with the 1956 New York Giants, right up to Cullen Jenkins, who won the Super Bowl with the Green Bay Packers in 2011.

Each player had a fascinating story to tell, and I wanted you to be able to read it in *their own words.* You see, I've written nearly 50 sports books, and for this series in particular, I wanted the players' quotes to be uninhibited, unfiltered, and raw. I wanted you to hear their stories from them directly, in the first person, without my voice polluting their thoughts and memories. It's anecdotal by design, and I hope you will enjoy the format. Look, I'm not winning any Pulitzers here, folks; most of my books wind up in bathrooms rather than coffee tables… and I'm okay with that, just as long as they get read. If you're a football fan, you'll like the book—it's a lot of fun—especially if your team is in here. If you're a Packer, Steeler, Cowboy, or 49er fan, I'm insanely jealous and I hate you. As for *my* team? Funny you should ask…. Sadly, my Minnesota Vikings are 0–4 when it comes to Super Bowls, so I suppose I'm going to have to keep drinking the purple Kool-Aid and hoping for the best. Hopefully in my lifetime, *please God*, that's all I'm gonna say. To better understand my true feelings, I would invite you to read *I Love Brett Favre – I Hate Brett Favre*, which I wrote in 2009. It's about my bipolar dysfunctional relationship with No. 4 and how he was supposed to bring me a Super Bowl but instead brought me more misery. But I digress….

As for my motive in writing the book? I wanted to find out why each team won. I wanted to dig down and find out what was so special about *that* team. I could only ask players about *that* championship season, nothing else. I started out asking the players what it meant to them to win the championship. The responses were humbling, thought-provoking, and intensely emotional. Next I asked them *why* that particular team won, and I wanted them to get specific. Real specific. The responses here were interesting, fascinating, and insightful. From there, I asked them if there was a defining moment from that season; a big win, a big loss, an off-the-field incident, a catalyst of some sort that got the momentum swinging their way and ultimately led them to the title. The responses here were intriguing, surprising, and even hilarious. Once I had that information, I wanted to better understand just how the coach from that team was able to get the job done. The responses here were all about leadership, motivation, and team building. As I learned, each coach had his own unique philosophy on how he was going to get from point A to point B, and no two were the same. Finally, I wanted to know what the big takeaway was from each individual. I wanted them to put the wisdom they had learned from winning a championship into a practical business application. I wanted them to share at least one life lesson that we, as readers, could take away and apply to our own lives. The responses here ranged from simple to profound to downright inspiring.

The journey of putting this all together was nothing short of incredible. I am a working member of the media with the Vikings, so fortunately I had great access to the players and coaches. Thanks to all of them who gave me their time and shared with me so many heartfelt stories about what it takes to reach the pinnacle of professional football success. It was a one-year odyssey of sorts in which I got to meet some pretty amazing people. Some stories about how players were able to overcome adversity and injuries were poignant, while others about how players were able to overcome racism and prejudices were riveting. From visiting with Steve Young on the sideline of a *Monday Night Football* game; to spending an afternoon with Howard Schnellenberger in his office at Florida Atlantic University; to hanging out with Leslie Frazier and Mike Singletary at the Vikings' corporate offices; to hitting the links with Bob Stein at the NFL Alumni Association's Golf Classic; to chatting over the phone with Art Donovan, the crusty old Baltimore Colts tackle, who shared some wonderfully filthy stories about what the NFL was like back in the '50s—each interview was a wonderful experience that added something unique to the book.

As for the history of the book's namesake, that beautiful sterling silver Lombardi Trophy, that too is an interesting story. You see, starting back in 1933, when the NFL began its playoff system, the winning team received the aforementioned Ed

Thorp Memorial Trophy. Thorp, a respected referee and rules expert, died that year, and a traveling trophy was created in his honor. Each championship team got their name inscribed on the trophy and then got to keep it for the upcoming season. When the NFL-AFL merger was ultimately completed in 1969, however, a new "World Professional Football Championship" trophy was created in its place by famed jeweler Tiffany & Co. The last NFL team to have its name etched onto it was the Minnesota Vikings, who won the NFL championship that season but then lost to the Chiefs in Super Bowl IV. In 1970, legendary Green Bay Packers coach Vince Lombardi, winner of the first two Super Bowls, tragically died from cancer. Wanting to honor his legacy, the championship trophy was officially renamed in his memory. The following season, the Vince Lombardi Trophy was presented to the Baltimore Colts after they defeated the Dallas Cowboys, 16–13, in Super Bowl V. Today it's presented by the commissioner to the winning owner and coach on the field following each Super Bowl.

One thing I found out along the way was that the old guys, for the most part, were all envious of the younger guys who actually got to hoist that beautiful Lombardi Trophy over their heads out on the field after winning the championship. "Back in the day" that was simply unheard of. And they were *all* insanely jealous of the NHLers who get to party like rock stars with the Stanley Cup for a day back in their hometowns while drinking cold adult beverages out of it. Memo to the NFL: you need to let your players take the Lombardi Trophy back home for a day and let them say thank you to all the people who helped them along the way. It's amazing P.R., and it's quite frankly the coolest tradition in sports. Look into it, Commish; your players want to start a new tradition, and this one would be epic. And given all the bad P.R. your league has endured over this past "locked out" 2011 off-season, you could use all the good mojo you can get. *Capiche?* Truth be told, some of your employees are already doing it. That's right. In fact, when Saints head coach Sean Payton won it in 2010, he took it home and slept with it.

"This thing lay in my bed next to me last night," he said. "I rolled over a couple of times. I probably drooled on it. But man, there's nothing like it."

My goal is to entertain, inform, and enlighten you. To take you behind the scenes and let you in on some facets of the game that have always intrigued me. My caveat to you is that I don't claim to be an expert, just a megafan with a passion for the game of football. *Yes*, I did play the game, though. In fact, I was an all-conference guard/defensive end in high school and even had offers to play Division II ball. Full disclosure: I opted to walk on to the University of Minnesota's top-ranked Golden Gophers hockey team instead and wound up becoming the team mascot, "Goldy the Gopher," after I got cut. Sadly, that was as far as I made it in big-time sports! Being a mischievous rodent actually got me into my first Super Bowl, though, back in 1992 at Super Bowl XXVI in Minneapolis, when I was asked to work the crowd as part of the halftime festivities. That was as close as I will ever get in my lifetime to "Raising Lombardi," but what a blast that was to be down on the field and to be a part of the action. The pomp and circumstance, the spectacle of the Super Bowl, it's truly larger than life. From the millions of dollars it costs to buy a 30-second commercial to the millions of fans who tune in around the world—it truly is the greatest show on Earth.

Sadly, ironically, and perhaps inappropriately, I want to leave you with a final thought. Err... rather, a conspiracy theory regarding my beloved Minnesota Vikings. Yes, I'm an unabashed homer, and I make no apologies for that. Anyway, as I mentioned earlier, the Ed Thorp Memorial Trophy was last awarded to the Purple People Eaters in 1969. Interestingly, that was the last anybody has ever seen of it. Ever. As in, it's lost. Gone. Missing. Maybe the World Professional Football

Championship trophy was created by necessity? Maybe they needed a new trophy because the other one was pilfered? Stolen? Swindled? Or maybe horribly misplaced? I guess what I'm trying to say here is that maybe we've been cursed. How else can you explain it? Look, in addition to four, yes four, Super Bowl losses, we've also lost four, yes, four, NFC Championship Games since then. Just how can that be?

I mean, what if Darrin Nelson's game-tying dropped pass from Wade Wilson against Washington with just 56 seconds left in the 1987 NFC Championship Game wasn't his fault? What if Gary Anderson's only missed field goal of the season that cost us the 1998 NFC Championship Game wasn't his fault? What if losing to the Giants by the narrow margin of 41–0 in the 2000 NFC Championship Game was just a fluke? And what if Brett Favre's last-second interception in the 2009 NFC Championship Game wasn't really his fault? Think about it. Maybe, just maybe, there was something else a little more sinister and mysterious going on. What if (just go with me on this one…) the ghost of Ed Thorp, lost somewhere in the Land of 10,000 Lakes all these years later, is still haunting us? I guess what I'm trying to say is this: whoever has the Ed Thorp Memorial Trophy sitting in his basement collecting dust, please give it back. Let's end this horrible hex. Look what happened in Boston when the Red Sox traded Babe Ruth: the "Curse of the Bambino" cost them nearly a century of heartache!

Okay, maybe that's a stretch, but I would like to see my Vikings win it just once in my lifetime. It's bad enough I have to listen to the cheeseheads rub it in after they just won their 13th championship. That's right, that's nine NFL championships and four Super Bowls for those keeping score at home. If you're a Minnesota fan, that really sucks. Okay, back to the "curse." It's gotta end, someway, somehow. It's like I can date my entire life around this team's futility. I was born in 1969, the year of their first Super Bowl loss. Look, I was only six years old when Dallas beat my Vikes in the divisional playoffs back in 1975, but I can still remember it like it was yesterday. How crazy is that? I can't even recall a birthday party until I was like 12, yet I remember crap like this? I remember watching the game in our basement and seeing my dad and two brothers going ballistic when Drew Pearson miraculously caught the game-winning touchdown from Roger Staubach after clearly pushing off cornerback Nate Wright. And yes, he *did* push off. They would call it the "Hail Mary." Needless to say, we had *another* name for that catch in our house, one that wasn't so righteous. The fans went nuts. One drunk lunatic even heaved a whiskey bottle off of the third deck of old Metropolitan Stadium and hit the referee in the head just moments after the big play. Luckily it didn't kill the guy, but if it had, I think a lot of folks up here would have considered it to be justifiable homicide. I even remember hearing afterward about how Fran Tarkenton's dad, whose name was ironically Dallas, tragically dropped dead of a heart attack while watching the game on TV. You just can't make this stuff up. Do the math, we're cursed.

So now I'm reduced to just rooting for Buffalo and Denver. That's right. That's how pathetic I've become. I now find myself rooting for those two to win the AFC championship and make it to the Super Bowl. Year in and year out, I want them to get there, I really do. Then, once they're there, I want them to lose. Badly. You see, I want somebody else to hold the dubious distinction of "Most Super Bowl Losses." The Bills lost four in a row from 1990 to 1993. Welcome to the club. Denver was right there with us too, having lost four from 1977 to 1989. But then John Elway somehow found the fountain of youth and led them to a pair of titles in '97 and '98. Whatever, dude. Hey, I'm desperate. So, go Bills and go Broncos! Until you make it to the Super Bowl, that is. I need one of you to come through for me and notch that coveted fifth loss. No hard feelings, it's not personal. I know you understand my pain.

So that's it. Dive in, relax, and enjoy. I hope you enjoy reading about all of these amazing champions half as much as I enjoyed writing about them. Cheers!

Being a Champion

Winning the championship is the pinnacle of football success, and when it happens the players' emotions simply take over. In this chapter I wanted to find out just what it meant for them to win it all and to finally become a champion. Each player's journey to get to that point is unique. When the reality of living out a childhood dream finally comes true, however, the emotion is raw, and the tears begin to flow freely. Some laughed, some cried, and some were just still too numb to feel anything. Yes, it was *that* profound.

WHAT DID IT MEAN FOR YOU TO WIN A CHAMPIONSHIP?

"It's what you play for. Under Lombardi's reign, that was the only goal that you had, to win that final game. I was fortunate enough to be on two Super Bowl teams in Green Bay, and it meant a great deal. The Packers have a very rich history of winning, and that really motivated us to win."

Donny Anderson
RB/P, Green Bay Packers, 1966, 1967

"It meant a great deal. I had played in Super Bowl I and lost, so to get a second chance at it and win it, that was a very special and proud moment in my life. We were so determined not to lose it again; we really wanted to redeem ourselves. We had such a great team that year. We had seven Hall of Famers on that team, and there should be a couple more as well. We had a great defense too, one of the best of all time in my book. No doubt about it, we were *that* good. We all believed in each other too; we really had each other's backs out there. You don't see that all the time in professional sports, but we had that type of camaraderie on that team. Because our defense was that good, we knew that if the offense could hang in there and put up some points, then we would do the rest. We knew that nobody was going to blow us out, so they were going to be close games.

We had to overcome a lot of adversity that year as well. Our quarterback, Len Dawson, got hurt and missed half the season. Mike Livingston played great as his backup though, and it was because of him that we were even in a position to get into the playoffs. So, that was huge for us. We hung on though and made it to the playoffs as a wild-card. From there we had to get past the defending champion Jets in the first round, which was no easy task. I will never forget that game out in New York—it was just a classic. I was so determined to do whatever I could to help my team win. I was a man possessed. I wound up making a couple of big plays, including stuffing [Jets quarterback] Joe Namath on a goal-line bootleg, and was awarded with the game ball afterward. That was a huge honor. Winning that game gave us a whole lot of momentum, and we used that to beat Oakland the next week. Oakland had already beaten us twice that season, but we dug in and took care of business.

*Bobby Bell eyes a Minnesota Vikings opponent during Super Bowl IV.
Bell's Kansas City Chiefs defeated the Minnesota Vikings 23–7.
(Focus On Sport/Getty Images)*

Next up were the big bad Purple People Eaters from
Minnesota, who we met up with down in New Orleans.
We were 14-point underdogs to those guys—talk about
feeling disrespected! They thought they were gonna come
in and dominate us, and we were not going to have any
part of that. We were hungry and just took it to 'em. We
played a complete game: offense, defense, and special
teams. We scored three quick field goals, and then Mike

Garrett scored on a short touchdown run to make it 16–0. Lenny Dawson hit Otis Taylor for a long touchdown late in the game and wound up being named as the MVP of the game. We won, 23–7, and it was pretty amazing. We just believed in ourselves and did it, that's why we earned the right to be Super Bowl champions.

One of the big regrets I have about the Super Bowl came afterward. I had to leave early the next morning with several of my teammates to play in the AFL All-Star Game, which used to be played immediately after the Super Bowl. So we wound up missing the parade and the parties and all of that fun stuff back in Kansas City. Honestly, had I known I was going to miss all of that stuff, I never would have agreed to play in it. I was so dead tired that next day, all I wanted to do was sit back and enjoy my ride in the parade."

Bobby Bell
DE, Kansas City Chiefs, 1969

"What it means to win an NFL championship is difficult to describe unless you've been through it. I've been on both sides of that fence too, so I would know. I was fortunate enough to win two championships as a player with Baltimore in 1958 and 1959 but then lost one as the head coach of the New England Patriots in 1985 to the Chicago Bears. That was tough. Trust me, winning it is a whole lot better than losing it, that's for sure. To win it is special though. That first one, in '58, it seemed like we didn't come down to earth for several months because it was such a high. It was the pinnacle of your football career, that was for sure. It was just a mountaintop experience, so memorable.

The 1958 championship was historic too, that's why it's now referred to as 'The Greatest Game.' It was so close, right down to the wire. We beat the Giants, 23–17, at Yankee Stadium. Then, on top of that, it went into overtime—which was completely new at that point. Nobody had ever really seen overtime before and didn't really know what it was. That threw a whole different angle on the whole thing; it was so unexpected and so unforgettable. The Giants had a very solid football team. Jim Lee Howell was their head coach, but Vince Lombardi ran their offense, and Tom Landry ran their defense, so to say they were well led would be quite an understatement.

I remember Frank Gifford putting them ahead early in the fourth quarter, but we came back to tie it with about two minutes left in the game. Unitas drove us down with just a few seconds to go, and we were able to tie it on a field goal that sent it to overtime. It was the first overtime game in NFL playoff history. Once the game ended, we all just stood there, expecting it to be a tie, and then the officials said that they were going to flip a coin to see who got the ball in sudden death. New York got the ball first, but we forced them to punt and then proceeded to drive the length of the field. We really wore them down. We then capped the win when Alan Ameche scored on a one-yard touchdown. It was an unbelievable feeling, truly.

Author's Note: Incidentally, during overtime, with the Colts on the Giants 8-yard line and poised to score, a fan ran out onto the field and forced a delay. It would later be revealed that the fan was actually an employee of NBC who had been "ordered to create a distraction because the national television feed had gone dead." Sure enough, by the time they caught the guy and got him off the field, they were able to fix the problem without missing any of the action. Berry, meanwhile, recorded a record 12 receptions for 178 yards and a touchdown in the win.

We won it again the next year too, 31–16, this time at Memorial [Stadium in Baltimore]. The '59 title game was actually very close until one key play midway through the game. The defining moment in it came when Johnny Unitas went back to pass, only to see that his No. 1 and No. 2 receivers were both covered. So, he scrambled and drilled Lenny Moore, our No. 3 receiver, on a slant pass, and he busted loose for a 60+ yard touchdown that broke the game open. That was the turning point in the game, no doubt about it. It was a heckuva game though, that was for sure.

I think to fully understand why we won those two magical seasons, you have to first go back and look at the 1957 season. We were in our third year of coming together as a team that season and had been gaining confidence. I think a defining moment for us that season came on our West Coast swing, where we lost to both the Rams and the 49ers. It really stung—. I mean our guys were very upset. To lose two games that we never should have lost got to us, and we channeled that frustration the following season. And even though we didn't make it to the championship game, we felt that we were better than both of the finalists, Detroit and Cleveland. So, we came into training camp that next season with a whole bunch of confidence and with a real aware-ness that we could in fact go all the way."

Raymond Berry
WR, Baltimore Colts, 1958, 1959

"It meant everything. That was what I played my football career for—an opportunity to win a championship. So, raising the Lombardi Trophy meant that I was now officially a champion. As soon as I could, I grabbed it and kissed it and raised it up to the fans in Detroit, my hometown. That was where I was born and raised, so that was my way of saying thanks to all of those people who had supported me through the years. I wanted to make sure that they had a chance to see it in my hands, up close and personal. I wanted them to share in my proudest moment as a player. You know, I think I had 40-some friends and family there, so not only was it a special day for me, it was an expensive day for me. Trust me, I played for free that day! Whatever Super Bowl bonus money I made that day, it went for tickets! For me, though, winning that game in Detroit against the Seahawks, that also meant that the journey was over. I retired right then and there out on the field, while I was holding that beautiful trophy.

We had lost in the AFC Championship Game the year before, and I was so bummed out after that. I just did not want my career to end on that note so I decided to come back for one more season and give it one last try. Thank God I did. I wanted to go out as a champion, and fortunately that was how it all worked out. It was everything that I had ever dreamed of. It was the perfect culmination of a career. I was finally able to achieve the ultimate goal that I had never been able to attain prior to that. So, for me it was really a special moment on a lot of different levels.

Once we got to the AFC Championship Game, my teammates were using my potential homecoming as their rallying cry. They wanted to get to Detroit so I could go out on top—that was pretty neat. They wanted to take me home, and that was our mantra, "We gotta take the Bus home…." I still get goose bumps thinking about it. One of the funniest things I remember about that day happened right before the game when we all ran out onto the field. Usually we all run out together as a team, but since I was from Detroit, Joey Porter pulled me aside right before we were set to go out there and told me that he wanted me to lead us out. I said

'Okay, no problem.' He said he would be right behind me. I figured, cool, this would be fun. So, I went flying out there, trying to fire up my teammates, fully expecting them to be right behind me. Only when I looked back, they were nowhere to be seen. I was like, 'Oh my God, what do I do?' I looked back into the tunnel and could see them all in there, and I was like, 'Come on…please!' Finally, they came running out there, and all I could do was laugh. Looking back, it was pretty special to be out there all alone like that, but I never would have done it had I known that they were going to pull that on me. I remember though, just looking up in the stands and feeling so proud to be back in my hometown. I will never forget that moment for as long as I live. To see all those Terrible Towels, I just knew that we were going to win that day.

My most memorable moment from the Super Bowl was turning out the lights in the locker room after everybody else had left. I ran across the street and did an interview with Jimmy Kimmel right after the game and didn't get back until late. So, by the time I got showered up everybody was gone. I was the last guy in there, and it was really symbolic of my career, because my career was over at that point. I was turning off the lights. It was a magical season and something I will never forget. What a ride."

Jerome Bettis
RB, Pittsburgh Steelers, 2005

"What does winning it mean? I think the biggest thing is the way that people perceive you now, after you have won it. People have asked me how my life has changed since winning it. I think about it, and I still approach every day the exact same way, and my priorities are still the same. I feel like the same person; I don't feel like I am doing any-thing differently. Yet, the way people talk to you, talk about you, just perceive you overall is different. I think that there is a higher level of respect." [1]

Drew Brees
QB, New Orleans Saints, 2009

"The best part of it for me is the idea that this group of young men, who came together and believed in them-selves, bought the team concept completely, took the names off the back of the jerseys, checked the egos at the door. The reinforcement for team is the greatest source of satis-faction for me. I told the players last night—and I had stayed away from any personal refrain because I didn't think it was proper timing, but last night it was. I told them about my experience in 1990, when you realize that you are the world champion. Other than your family and your children and those type of things, professionally, there is no comparison to the feeling. You could walk around six feet high, and it would be appropriate for our players. When you stop and think about Michael Strahan, when you stop and think about Jeff Feagles; Jeff in his 20th year and only six times in the playoffs. You start to think about all our vet-eran guys who now are world champions and are experi-encing that feeling for the first time, reinforcing the concept of team, that's the greatest thing for me." [2]

Tom Coughlin
Head Coach, New York Giants, 2007

"It was a childhood dream. I had watched that moment so many times before on TV, sitting on the couch, when the winning players all celebrate out on the field with all the confetti coming down. So, when it happened to me, it was totally surreal. I was just so proud of our guys. The way we overcame so many injuries and then won on the road in the playoffs, it was incredible. Then, to beat Pittsburgh the way we did, in such a thrilling game, I'll never forget it. The whole experience was just magical."

Mason Crosby
K, Green Bay Packers, 2010

"Even as a child I was obsessed with being a member of the best team. The New York Yankees were my favorite team as a kid because they were the best. As such, my dream was to pitch for the Yankees and win a World Series. I was consumed with that dream and spent all day every day pitching a baseball, constantly practicing. When I came up short as the starting pitcher for my College Park [Georgia] high school team at the state finals my junior year, I finally came to the realization that if I couldn't win there, then I was probably going to have a tough time against the Dodgers. So, I took up football instead. Not in my wildest dreams, however, did I think that I would be playing for the Green Bay Packers in the first-ever Super Bowl. What a feeling—it was incredible. We had actually won the NFL title the year before, so this made it back-to-back championships for me. It was such a thrill. What a privilege to play for Coach Lombardi and to be a part of such an incredible team. To have that sense of belonging to a group of individuals who were the greatest in the world, that was *it* for me. It was as if that childhood quest had been fulfilled. I would win another Super Bowl several years later with the Baltimore Colts, and believe it or not, that feeling of being the best has never left me. That's why I continue to coach today. I love teaching young people in the classroom and on the field about what it takes to not only be a loyal teammate, but about being the best. So, looking back, winning those championships was *huge* to that young Bill Curry. Just *huge*. Words can't describe how impactful it was on me. It was life changing, it really was."

Bill Curry

C, Green Bay Packers, 1965, 1966;
Baltimore Colts, 1970

"To any athlete, winning the championship is the ultimate. That's why you go to training camp. There's just nothing else like it. I was very fortunate to have won five of them over my career, three NFL championships and two Super Bowls, and that's something I'm extremely proud of. Winning them is incredible, but they're so rare. That's what makes them so special. I remember winning that first one against the Giants. What a feeling, I will never forget it. It was unbelievable. It's an accomplishment where there's just nothing else quite like it. We had come close the year before and lost to Philadelphia, and Coach Lombardi was so upset afterward. He basically guaranteed that we were going to get back and win it the next year, and sure enough we did.

Then, winning that first Super Bowl in '67, against the Chiefs, that was significant. It was the first head-to-head matchup between the established NFL and upstart AFL, and we wanted to beat those guys. We felt the pressure big time coming into that game. We knew that if we got beat that we would have *a lot* of explaining to do. The AFL teams felt that they were every bit as good as we were, but we felt we were better. So in our eyes, by beating them the way we did, 35–10, it kind of settled the argument. The

Chiefs had a great team though, but being the competitors that we were, we wanted to take it to them as best we could. Beating the Raiders the following season was just as sweet, down in Miami, to give the Packers the first two Super Bowls in history. Once you get that taste of winning, it's so hard to let go. I wanted more and more—what a feeling."

Willie Davis
DE, Green Bay Packers,
1961, 1962, 1965, 1966, 1967

Super Second Place

From 1960 through 1969, the NFL staged an additional postseason game the week after the NFL championship called the "Playoff Bowl" or "Runner-up Bowl" down in Miami at the Orange Bowl. These games matched the second-place teams from the two conferences and were advertised as third-place playoff games. The game was discontinued after the AFL-NFL merger with the final contest being played in January 1970.

"I was fortunate to have been able to win one as both a player and a coach, and that was pretty special. Winning championships, that's your lifetime goal, your ambition, that's why you play the game. I was lucky in that I was able to play on some great teams, alongside some great teammates, and for some great coaches. As a player, nothing is better than winning something together with your teammates, the guys you go to battle with. That's the ultimate. Then, as a coach, when you can be an architect and share a vision that can help put it all together, that's a tremendously rewarding feeling. Our goal in 1985 was to

win the Super Bowl, and when we did it, it was very satisfying. We had a great group of guys that season, and I
was really proud of them. It was so rewarding because we
fulfilled our expectations."

Mike Ditka
TE, Dallas Cowboys, 1971;
Head Coach, Chicago Bears, 1985

"What a team we had in those days. To go back-to-back
was something else. The first one was in 1958, when we
beat the Giants in overtime, 23–17, at Yankee Stadium. It
was so sweet to beat the Giants that year. We didn't even
realize it at the time that it would be called 'The Greatest
Game Ever Played.' It was just another game to us that we
wanted to win. We didn't care about the trophy either; we
wanted that bonus check—it was like five thousand bucks,
which was almost more than our salaries in those days. For
me, winning that first one was extra special though
because I was born and raised just a few miles up the road
from Yankee Stadium in the Bronx. So, to beat those guys
in those hallowed grounds, where I used to watch so many
great ballplayers, it was something else. We beat them
again the next year too, 31–16, only this time it was at
Memorial Stadium in Baltimore. The first half was close,
but we beat the living hell out of them in the second half.
We were so tough. With a guy like John Unitas at quarterback, what more could you ask for? We just had a helluva
team, and I was so damn proud of my teammates. We
were the champs for two straight seasons, the best in the
business, and nobody could ever take that away from us.
The great thing about those two teams is that even now, in
2011, the fans in Baltimore still think that us guys who
played on those two teams can walk on water. It's just

wonderful the way they treat us. And don't think we don't all appreciate it, because we do. Those were wonderful times, they really were."

Art Donovan
DT, Baltimore Colts, 1958, 1959

"I've been very blessed in that I have been able to have been a part of two championship teams, one as a player and one as a head coach. As a player, I was a member of the '79 Pittsburgh Steelers and we beat the Dallas Cowboys that year, which was certainly the highlight of my playing career. Then what an awesome thrill it was for me to win it again as a coach, this time with the Indianapolis Colts in 2007 when we beat the Chicago Bears. Being the first African American coach to win it made it even more special because I felt I was representing a lot of guys who had gone before me. My perspective totally changed this time too. As a player, you're in the moment, and it's all so new and exciting. As a coach, you see everything that goes into it and what goes on behind the scenes from an organizational perspective. I can remember the clock winding down and knowing that we were going to win. I was thinking how special it was, knowing how hard it was just to get there. All that hard work, all that preparation, all that time, it finally all paid off. What a feeling."

Tony Dungy
DB, Pittsburgh Steelers, 1978;
Head Coach, Indianapolis Colts, 2006

"To raise that trophy, it was surreal. I remember having my picture taken with it and just thinking about how amazing that moment was. I had always wanted to play in the NFL as a kid, so to reach the pinnacle like that is almost beyond words. It's like you're living out a childhood dream. I had seen my brother win it in 1981, and how much it meant to him, and that really made me hungry. I had watched my big brother play with the team while I was still in college and was just in awe of the guys. So, when I got there after playing two seasons in the USFL, it was like I had died and gone to heaven. I remember sitting down in the locker room and thinking to myself, *Wow, there's Joe Montana, there's Dwight Clark, there's Jerry Rice, there's Roger Craig, there's Ronnie Lott, there's Dwight Hicks, there's Eric Wright, there's Hacksaw Reynolds,* and on and on. It was just a who's who of star players I had sort of grown up idolizing. So, to win it and to be a part of that fraternity, it's almost beyond words.

As for the games themselves? I won three Super Bowl rings but only got to play in one of the games. I missed playing in 1985 because my body simply gave out. You see, I had played in the USFL [a rival league] that spring and then joined the Niners when that season ended. I had a whopping two weeks off and then headed right back into training camp. Well, all that wear and tear eventually took a toll, and I blew my knee out in Week 14 while playing in my 38th overall game of the year. How's that for crazy? I was a noodle that season, getting shot up in my foot, quad, and ribs before games. I was a mess, just totally beat up. Then, to have to go up against opposing players who were juicing in those days, and were just strong as hell, it was nuts. Looking back, I think playing that many games in one season probably took two or three years off of my career. It was insane.

Anyway, we beat the Dolphins in the Super Bowl that year, 38–16, but having to miss it really sucked. My brother

Keith got to play though, so at least one of us got to be out there representing the family. It was pretty cool to be team-mates with my brother that year. That was something we both really treasure. Ironically, because I was in a cast at the time though, the coaches didn't want me on the side-line—for fear of me getting injured. So I wound up watch-ing the game with my wife in the hospital room of Keith's wife, who was pregnant and about to give birth. I figured that as long as he couldn't be there, then I would fill in for him. Hey, I know he'd do the same for me!

I started the next one though, Super Bowl XXIII, where we beat Cincinnati, 20–16, down in Miami. That was pretty amazing. We made it back the next year too, where we beat Denver, 55–10, only I was on the shelf there as well with a broken foot. So, you just never know in this busi-ness. I was certainly a part of all three teams, but certainly the second one means the most in that it was the only one where I actually got to start and contribute to my team's success. It was the best game of all three too, that was 'The Drive,' where Joe Montana brought us back 92 yards in the last two minutes to win it. It was epic, just incredible. The Bengals didn't know what hit them. Joe was a very quiet leader. He didn't talk much, but when he did every-body just shut up and listened. He led by example, that was his style. As his teammate, you just always knew that you could count on him. The guy delivered. You certainly can't argue with the results; he's arguably the best ever."

Jim Fahnhorst
LB, San Francisco, 1984, 1988, 1989

"Winning the Super Bowl is like 10 times better than any-thing you ever could have imagined. It's that good. Just the satisfaction of realizing you were a part of the best team in the world that year is almost overwhelming. To know that you have reached the pinnacle in your career, what we all strive for in this game, is an incredible feeling, just totally surreal. I was fortunate to have won two Super Bowls, and I wear my two rings proudly every day. Whenever I look

San Francisco offensive tackle Keith Fahnhorst looks on from the sideline during the 49ers' 38–16 win over the Miami Dolphins in Super Bowl XIX. Fahnhorst was a member of two 49ers Super Bowl teams. (Michael Zagaris/Getty Images)

down at them, regardless of what I am doing, I always think back to those two magical seasons and about all the hard work and sacrifice that it took to earn them."

Keith Fahnhorst

OT, San Francisco 49ers, 1981, 1984

"As a player, it was a dream come true. For me, to have grown up in Mississippi and then to have been a part of one of the most celebrated football teams in history, the '85 Bears, it was special in so many ways. As a player, you practice and prepare your whole life to be a Super Bowl champion. So when it happens, it's extremely gratifying. Just to make it to the National Football League is an amazing achievement, but to become a member of a world championship team, that's an entirely different level.

For me, winning the Super Bowl was one of the greatest days of my life, as well as one of the worst. I had injured my knee midway through the game, and sadly it turned out to be my last ever as a player. I remember sitting there with the trainers at halftime, and they said that I wouldn't be able to go back out there. And then, to make matters worse, I wound up missing the celebration in the locker room afterward because I was in a meeting with the doctor. I had dreamt about that moment for so long too, popping champagne bottles and high-fiving my teammates. I could actually hear them down the hall from where I was, but I couldn't be a part of it. So, my emotions were mixed.

Truth be told, I didn't even want to go to the team party that evening, but my wife made me. I came in on crutches, and everybody was celebrating. Guys were coming up to me, asking me how I was doing. They were so excited, so proud of what we had accomplished. You could just see guys, so happy, saying, 'We did it! We did it!' I was so bummed out because I wanted to be jumping around, having a good time, but all I could think about was the operation I was about to have. So, it was a jubilant time, as well as a somber time for me. I knew though that if that was going to be my last game ever, that it was a heckuva way to go out. At least I was going out on top, and for that I feel very fortunate. Not a lot of people know this, but I have never watched that play, ever, even after all these years. I just don't want to relive it; it's just too painful to think about.

The silver lining to me suffering a career-ending injury I suppose was that I was able to get into coaching after that. It set me out on another career path with new goals and aspirations. So, when I was able to win another Super Bowl, this time as an assistant coach with the Colts in 2007, that's something that I am also extremely proud of. I'm so grateful to Tony [Dungy, head coach] for the opportunity to be a part of that team. And what an amazing moment that was, to experience that feeling of what it was like to be a champion all over again—this time out on the field with the guys.

Tony was such a great leader, and everybody wanted to win that championship for him. He had been so close prior to that and had always fallen short, so this was *his* time. We wanted to get him over the top so badly; that became our mission that season, our focus. He set the tone early on and created an atmosphere where you were never really overly concerned from game to game about what the outcome was going to be. Tony was really able to get the players to buy into his message. He was very calm and very consistent with the way he delivered his message too.

For instance, I remember late that season we got beaten pretty badly by the Jacksonville Jaguars, 44–17. They humiliated us, just ran the football up and down the field on our defense—it was embarrassing. After the game the media were all over Tony. They were basically writing us off, figuring we could never recover from a loss like that so late in the season. They wanted to know if he was going to make any changes and what he was going to do moving forward. Well, Tony stood in front of the entire team very calmly and told us that we weren't going to change a thing. He told us that we were going to work a little bit harder on some things and just try to improve for the next week. He reassured us and told us not to panic and that we were going to be just fine. It was amazing. Most head coaches would never say that kind of stuff to their team after such a bad loss, but Tony had his own style. The players believed in him. I remember listening to some of our leaders at their press conferences the next day. Guys like Peyton Manning, they were saying the same exact thing that Tony had said in our team meeting after the game. 'We're not going to panic, we're not making lineup changes, we're going to work just a little bit harder, we're going to be just fine.' Wow! That's influence. That's leadership. Sure enough, everybody worked a little bit harder, and we went on to win that Super Bowl for Tony. It was incredible. Tony, of course, went through some personal tragedy the season before when he lost his son, so to see him so happy and on top of the world—it was extremely gratifying."

Leslie Frazier
CB, Chicago Bears, 1985;
Assistant Coach, Indianapolis Colts, 2006

"Winning the Super Bowl is the ultimate prize. It's the goal we all work toward in this business. So to achieve it is such a special feeling. Ever since I was a little kid I wanted to

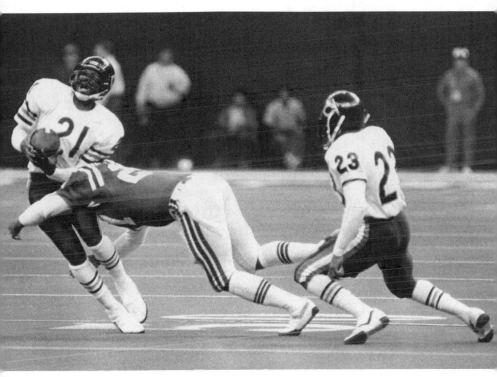

Chicago's Leslie Frazier carries the ball during Super Bowl XX. The Bears defeated the New England Patriots, 46–10, but Frazier suffered a career-ending knee injury on a punt return in the second quarter. Frazier earned a second Super Bowl ring as the Indianapolis Colts' defensive backs coach when the Colts defeated the Bears in Super Bowl XLI. (Jonathan Daniel/Getty Images)

win the Super Bowl. My journey to winning it was certainly unique. I had played with the Carolina Panthers that entire 2007 season and then became a free agent. The Giants picked me up after they beat Tampa Bay in the playoffs, at which point I joined their roster. I only played on the practice squad that postseason; that was it. I was there on the sideline with my jersey on, but sadly I never got into the game. It still meant a lot to be a part of the team though and to share in the victory. I was able to bring my family down for the game, which was really special too. In fact, my grandfather, who I was very close to, had just passed away prior to the game, and I know that he was watching over us as our guardian angel—making sure we played well and took care of business. That was special to think about that and to be able to share that moment with my family, who had supported me for so many years.

As for the game itself, it was pretty memorable. We were underdogs that entire postseason but just found a way to get it done. We won every playoff game on the road and then upset one of the best teams in NFL history, the New England Patriots—who had come into the game unde-feated. It was an amazing game, so exciting and with such a dramatic ending with David Tyree making that incredible catch off his helmet from Eli Manning. That was such a defining moment for the team; they really fed off of that—you could just feel it on the sideline, how the momentum swung in our favor after that. It will go down in Super Bowl history as one of the greatest plays of all time. I think the big takeaway for me through it all is that sometimes you gotta be in the right place at the right time. Luckily the Giants picked me up that year, and I just got to ride the wave from there. Hey, I'm a Super Bowl champion, and they can't ever take that away from you. It was just a great experience and something I will never forget."

Marcus Freeman
TE, New York Giants, 2007

"I had always had great success throughout my career in athletics, but I had never really won anything. So, to finally become a champion was a really special moment for me. We beat the Minnesota Vikings to win it, and they were heavily, heavily favored to win that game. We were the underdogs coming in against those Purple People Eaters, and we stuck it to 'em pretty good. Winning that game was for sure the highlight of my playing career."

Mike Garrett
RB, Kansas City Chiefs, 1969

"The Super Bowl is the pinnacle of why you play. The year before we had gotten beaten in the Super Bowl, and in 1966 and '67 we had lost to Green Bay in the championship game. So, to get there is a big deal and very difficult, but to win it is the ultimate. It's what all football players strive for. And hey, that bonus check was nice too. In fact, I went out and bought a new horse afterward with it. I named him '98.' He was a good horse too, really fast. You see, I truly was a cowboy. My off-season occupation was riding in rodeos, steer wrestling, roping, and whatnot, so to be a champion Cowboy had a dual meaning for me."

Walt Garrison
RB, Dallas Cowboys, 1971

"Winning the championship, that was the ultimate. It was what we all strived for. That '56 championship was my only one, so it's very special. Sadly, I was on several teams that lost the championship after that. We lost back-to-back titles in '58 and '59 to Baltimore and then lost three in a row to Green Bay and Chicago from '61 to '63. That was tough. To get there that many times, five times in six years, and not come away with it, it was tough. Losing that '58 game was probably the toughest of all of them; that was 'The Perfect Game,' where we lost in the final moments to Johnny Unitas and the Colts. It was one of the first nationally televised sporting events, so for a lot of folks it was their first taste of pro football. It amazes me even to this day how many people still love to talk about that game.

Anyway, the NFL in the '50s was nothing like it is today though, nothing. This was a totally different era. I didn't grow up thinking about how great the NFL was; in fact, I had hardly even ever heard of it. I was on my way up to go skiing at Mt. Baldy in San Bernardino when I heard on the radio that I had been drafted No. 1 by the Giants. I remember thinking, *Why in the world would a baseball team draft me?* Seriously, the NFL was not the big deal back then like it is today. I was really taken aback by it. I didn't know who coached them or anything. I grew up in Southern California and had been familiar with the Rams, so I thought if I ever played, it would be with them, but I had no idea who even played for the Giants. To be honest, I wasn't terribly interested in playing anyway because it wasn't a very big deal to play pro football in 1952. It wasn't glamorous then like it is today. No one really cared much about it or paid much attention to it. College football was what people cared about and, of course, Major League Baseball.

I had just studied acting at USC and was interested in pursuing that line of work. I had even been working as an extra and as a stuntman in Hollywood, but I figured I would give football a shot. We had played Army my senior year in Yankee Stadium, and I got a taste of New York City, which really intrigued me. I remember going to a Broadway show and seeing Times Square; it was pretty exciting to me. I later learned that the reason the Giants selected me was because I had a good game against Army that day, and [Giants owner] Wellington Mara was there and saw me. He drafted me No. 1 without even ever meeting me. That's how primitive it was in those days. I had gotten married my senior year and figured we would spend a year in New York having fun, going to the theater. Who'd a thunk I'd still be here all these years later?"

Frank Gifford
HB, New York Giants, 1956

New York Giants running back Frank Gifford scores a touchdown during the 1956 NFL Championship Game at Yankee Stadium. The Giants defeated the Chicago Bears, 47–7. (Bruce Bennett Studios/Getty Images)

Titletown, USA

The Green Bay Packers are the NFL's most successful franchise, winning 13 titles during the league's history. Green Bay also holds the distinction of winning the most NFL titles in the pre-Super Bowl era with nine. While the Pack has won four Super Bowls, it's the Pittsburgh Steelers who hold the record for most Super Bowl victories with a total of six.

"To win that first Super Bowl was special. It was almost a relief in many respects because we all knew how important it was for Lombardi to win it. That was the first year that the NFL played the AFL for the championship, and the pressure was on for us to beat those guys."

Gale Gillingham
G, Green Bay Packers, 1966, 1967

"It can't be put into words. Every team that I have ever played on, in football, basketball, or whatever, the goal is to always win the championship. To win it all is what it's all about; that's your goal at the beginning of the season. So to see that become a reality is really an amazing feeling. I had never been able to win a championship until I went to Green Bay and Vince Lombardi came to town. Once Vince arrived, everything changed. We lost the championship to Philadelphia in 1960, and Vince was not happy about that whatsoever. Losing that game really drove him, made him hungry. We won it the next year, and we would go on to win a total of three championships and two Super Bowls over the next eight years. How's that for a dynasty?"

Forrest Gregg
OT, Green Bay Packers,
1961, 1962, 1965, 1966, 1967

"For me it meant a great deal, especially winning that first one. It meant so much to our organization to get that first title in '74. Pittsburgh had always been known as a losing franchise up until that point, with teams that were known for playing tough, hard-nosed football but couldn't make big plays in the fourth quarter and just couldn't get over that hump. So, when we got that first championship, it was such a relief. To see the look on Mr. Rooney's face, our longtime owner and really one of the NFL's founding fathers, it was extremely gratifying. Watching him hoist that Lombardi Trophy after we beat Minnesota down in New Orleans for that first one, and to see him get that monkey off his back, it was probably the highlight of my career to be honest. Then, to win three more over the next five years and create a dynasty the way we did during that era, it was very special."

Jack Ham
LB, Pittsburgh Steelers,
1974, 1975, 1978, 1979

"It's the next best thing from my son being born. That's what type of experience this is to me. It's just unbelievable the type of commitment, the type of sacrifice it took to achieve this." [3]

Rodney Harrison
CB, New England Patriots,
2003, 2004

"Winning the Super Bowl, that's what you work for every year. I had never won a postseason game prior to coming to the Raiders. So, when I finally won it, it was as if a huge weight had been lifted off of my shoulders. It was the only one I got during my 14-year career too, so when it finally happened for me it was pretty profound. What an awesome feeling of accomplishment. I just wish I could have experienced it a whole bunch more."

Mike Haynes
CB, Los Angeles Raiders, 1983

"Everybody who plays this game aspires to win the Super Bowl, that's what it's all about. You want to be a champion, the best of the best. I was fortunate to have won four of them over my career. My first one came in just my second year in the league with Baltimore [1971], and it was such an amazing experience. They had lost to the Jets two years earlier in the Super Bowl, and they were hungry. This was the transition from the old NFL to the new NFL, and the popularity of the game was exploding. It was just a huge honor to crack the starting lineup for that team because they had so much talent across the board there—guys like Johnny Unitas, John Mackey, and Tom Matte, to name a few. We wound up beating the Bengals and Raiders in the playoffs and then got past Dallas in the Super Bowl in a real tight game. I remember Jim O'Brien kicking the game-winning field goal in the game's final seconds. We ended up winning, 16–13, but it was so close. It was really an emotional battle, right up until the end. I'll never forget it.

From there, I was fortunate to win another three Super Bowls with the Raiders. The first one came in 1977, when

Raiders linebacker Ted Hendricks celebrates during the Raiders' 27–10 win over the Philadelphia Eagles in Super Bowl XV. (Bill Smith/ Getty Images)

we beat Minnesota. The Raiders had been so close so many times prior to that, even losing it in Super Bowl II, and they were determined to finally get it done. We had a great team, and it just all came together for us that year. We had only lost one game coming into the Super Bowl. We really wanted to win it for Coach Madden;

that became our focus. The media had really hounded him about how he had gotten his teams close so many times but that he was unable to win the big one. That really bothered us and became a big motivator for us. As for the game, it started out close, but we just pulled away from them late and won it convincingly, 32–14. They had a great defense with the 'Purple People Eaters,' but we dominated them. It was pretty incredible. I will never forget seeing Fran Tarkenton, their star quarterback, sitting on his helmet and crying after the game. It was surreal.

The second one came in 1981, when we beat Philadelphia down in New Orleans, 27–10. What was special about that team was the way that we got there. We were a wildcard that year and had to get past Cleveland and San Diego on the road to get there in the playoffs. I will never forget that game in Cleveland—it was bitter cold. To hear that crowd of 80,000 go silent when Mike Davis picked off Brian Sipe's pass, that was incredible. I had hit him from behind as he was releasing the ball. It was a pretty cool moment because I knew that the game was over at that point. We were the underdogs coming into the Super Bowl and kind of felt disrespected by that, so it turned out to be a pretty big motivator for us I think. That chip on our shoulder really drove us. The Eagles had beaten us earlier in the year, and we were hungry for payback. So, to win that one the way we did was extremely gratifying.

The third one with the Raiders was when we beat Washington down in Tampa in '84, but there were a lot of the same guys on the roster from the '81 team. This one was a blowout; we beat them 38–9. Our defense was so strong that game. I remember our two corners, Lester Hayes and Mike Haynes, they just blanketed the Redskins

wide receivers all day. They shut everybody down. Our
defensive line shut down their big fullback, John Riggins,
too. So, once we took away their air attack as well as their
ground attack, it was over. I remember Marcus Allen
breaking off that big run; that pretty much sealed the victory for us. That was my last one, and it was special, but
they all meant a great deal to me. To be a four-time Super
Bowl champion, hey, they can never take that away from
you. I can't say the same for the rings though, because my
kids have already taken those!"

Ted Hendricks
LB, Baltimore Colts, 1970;
Oakland Raiders, 1976, 1980;
Los Angeles Raiders, 1983

"My situation was a little unique. I was there in San Diego
when we beat the Broncos, 42–10 but, sadly, never got
onto the field. I actually blew my knee out three days before
the NFC Championship Game against Minnesota and
unfortunately never got to actually play in the Super Bowl.
To say I was bummed out would be quite an understatement. I was a rookie that season and had been playing as
a backup on the offensive line, in addition to all the special
teams. I was young and figured with the team we had that
we would be back to many more Super Bowls, so I just
focused on rehab and getting back out there. I figured,
heck, good offensive linemen can have long careers in this
league, 10–15 years, and this was just a minor setback.

Sure enough, I got back on the field six months later, ready
to help my teammates repeat as world champions. Then,
just two hours into my first minicamp practice back with my
teammates, I blew out my other knee while I was pivoting
on some old Astroturf. It was like a suction cup, grabbing

my foot, and didn't give as my body rolled over. It felt like a grenade went off in there—it was just brutal. In fact, it was a career ender for me, and regrettably I never got to play again. Needless to say, I was pretty devastated. To be a part of that 1987–88 team though, it was pretty special. Even though I didn't get to play in that game, I absolutely felt like I was a part of it and that I had contributed to the team's overall success. Absolutely.

What was unique about this team was that even though it was a strike year in 1987–88, we all stayed together. Nobody crossed the picket line. We all sat back and watched the replacement players, or 'scabs' as they were unaffectionately known, go 3–0. Well, those games counted, so that really helped us in the standings. So when we finally settled and got back out on the field, we were in first place and ready to go.

We had a great team with so many veteran leaders, guys like Dave Butz and of course the 'Hogs.' Those guys were great: Russ Grimm, Jeff Bostic, Joe Jacoby, they were sort of the first real celebrity offensive linemen in the league, and they couldn't have been more supportive and helpful to me. Doug Williams was our quarterback and was a great leader too. There were some characters too, guys like Dexter Manley and George Rogers, who were a lot of fun and kept things loose.

I will never forget riding in the parade down Constitution Avenue in downtown Washington, D.C., and then shaking President Reagan's hand in the White House. It was all pretty amazing. So, what does it mean? It means a great deal. Hey, a lot of guys play their whole careers and never get a sniff at it, and I was fortunate enough to have it in my one and only season in the league. You appreciate it more and more as you get older and wiser. I still wear that ring proudly today. Trust me, it opens a lot of doors and starts a lot of conversations."

Ray Hitchcock
G, Washington Redskins, 1987

"It meant a great deal at the time, but I think it means even more after you retire. While you're playing the game, championships and Super Bowls are what you play for. That's your goal, your expectation. Afterward, when you have time to sit back and reflect, that's when it kind of sinks in, and you can enjoy it and appreciate it a little more I think. To be a champion, that's a pretty special thing—and they can never take that away from you. No sir."

Paul Hornung
HB, Green Bay Packers,
1961, 1962, 1965, 1966

"There's only been 45 teams in NFL history who have won it, so it means a lot. It's historic. Just to be a contributor on such an incredible team, it's something that they can never take away from you. I will never forget getting to hold the Lombardi Trophy down on the field after the game along-side my family. Even though I never actually got a picture of it, it's something I will remember for the rest of my life. I just hope there will be many more chances to hold it again in the future."

Cullen Jenkins
DE, Green Bay Packers, 2010

"It feels great. To God be the glory. We overcame adversity all year. To go into halftime and find out that two of our leaders, Donald Driver and Charles Woodson, weren't going to be able to come back out, it just showed the poise that this team had and our will to overcome adversity. Winning the Super Bowl, it's the ultimate gratification. It's a dream come true. You play this game to get a ring. You play this game to be praised on Super Bowl Sunday with your teammates. So, for us to be in this situation, and the fact that we were able to overcome so much adversity, to God be the glory." [4]

Greg Jennings
WR, Green Bay Packers, 2010

"It meant everything. As a kid, I grew up dreaming of hoisting that trophy. I followed every inch of the game growing up. I was obsessed with it. So to see that dream come true was pretty amazing. It gives me chills when I think about it because it means that much to me, it really does. Having a deep understanding of the history and of all the great players who came before me, it's very humbling to be in that same group of champions. There have been so many unbelievable players and coaches over the years who have played this game for a very long time and have simply not had the chance to win one, and that just completely humbles me."

Brent Jones
TE, San Francisco 49ers,
1988, 1989, 1994

"Winning the Super Bowl was one of the greatest experiences of my life, truly a dream come true. We had been close several times in the previous five years but had come up short each time. The year before we lost to Baltimore in the championship game, and we just decided that this time around we were simply not going to be denied. I just think that this particular team had a special commitment and cohesiveness, which was totally unique. We had some really strong veteran leaders on that team too, which made a big difference in us winning it. To finally win it though, after all those years, it was beyond special."

Lee Roy Jordan
LB, Dallas Cowboys, 1971

"To fully understand what it meant, you have to come back with me to my hometown and hear the whole story. I grew up in a little town in northern Idaho, 3,500 people, a long way from the National Football League. I didn't have a television growing up, so I didn't know much about pro football to be honest. As a kid I enjoyed playing the game, but I had no dreams of ever playing beyond high school, and I certainly didn't think I would ever win a Super Bowl. I was pretty good in high school though, and that earned me a trip to college at the University of Idaho. That was an accomplishment in itself because going to college was something that nobody had ever done in my family up to that point. So it was a pretty big deal. Eventually, after playing college football for a while, and realizing that I was actually a pretty decent player, the NFL seemed like a real possibility.

When Green Bay drafted me in '58 I wasn't really sure what to think. They weren't winning a whole lot of big games in those days, and I was skeptical. When I got there it was kind of a wasteland. The coach at the time was a very nice man but certainly not very well qualified to coach at that level.

We were a pretty lousy football team when I got there; in fact, we had the worst record in the league. I remember playing a lot of poker with the guys, and I remember losing a lot of lopsided ballgames. We had some good ballplayers, but we just couldn't seem to beat anybody.

Everything changed, however, when Vince Lombardi came to town the following season. At first us players were skeptical of him. He had been an assistant with the Giants and didn't have any head coaching experience, other than in high school. We were pulling for Curly Lambeau, who actually wanted the job and was somebody we already liked and respected. I thought management was nuts to be honest. How could they pass on Curly and go with this unknown no-name? So, we headed back to training camp, not really knowing what to expect. We got there and played some golf and had some beers, figuring we would stroll into camp when the veterans showed up a few days later. Guys didn't show up in shape to camp in those days. We figured that was what the first few weeks were for, to kind of ease back into the swing of things. Vince didn't see it that way though, not by a long shot.

I remember coming out of my dorm room a day or two after I got back up there and walking down the stairs. I had my golf clubs over my shoulder, and I ran into Coach Lombardi. He looks right at me and screams, 'Where the hell do you think you're going?' I said very quietly, 'I'm gonna go play a little golf, Coach.' 'Like hell you are! Get back up there! You'll be at all meals, all meetings, and all practices—just like everybody else. Now go get dressed!'

That was my first introduction to Coach Lombardi. I was shocked. Who the hell was this guy, and who the hell did he think he was talking to? Well, I went and got dressed, and when I got out there for practice, Vince informed us that we would be having a couple extra days of two-a-days [tough off-season practices] just for good measure. He put us through hell. Our workouts were so intense, just brutal. Every drill was at high speed and with great intensity. We weren't allowed to walk from drill to drill; we ran, and we ran fast. We didn't know what had hit us to be honest. It didn't take us very long to figure out that this guy meant business. It was exhausting. Guys started bitching and moaning—they thought he was nuts. He didn't care. The more we bitched, the harder he pushed us. He told us that he had a philosophy and plan for us and that if we didn't like it, then we could get the hell out of there. He was intimidating and he was tough. God, he was tough.

Eventually though, we started to come around. It was a totally different approach that he had, and it didn't take us long to realize that this guy wanted to win. He was all about winning and winning *his* way. We went 7–5 his first season and made big improvements on both sides of the ball. The next season, however, we came into our own. The next year we all knew what to expect when we got to training camp, and it went a whole lot smoother. His system made more sense in year two, and we all understood how he wanted things done. We clicked and, as such, wound up making it to the NFL Championship Game against the Eagles. We played them tough but unfortunately came up short in the final seconds of the game, losing 17–13, over at Franklin Field in Philly. We felt like we should have won though. It was a controversial play at the end of the game, and Vince was really upset.

After the game though, for the first time, that was when I really started to believe in him. We were all bitching in the locker room, whining about how their game officials had not stopped the clock properly and ultimately gave them the win. We were all pissing and moaning about it. Vince then came into the locker room after talking to the press and huddled everybody together in the middle of the room. He hollered, 'Bring it up, everybody up!' We all came over, and he said very matter-of-factly, 'okay, this year we played in the championship. Next year we win the championship.' That was it. But you know what? He was exactly right. In fact, we not only won it the next season, we won it the one after that as well. I think Vince knew what the hell he was talking about!

By then we all thought that Vince walked on water. We respected him and would do just about anything for him. He had single-handedly transformed that entire organization from worst to first. It was incredible. He had such a passion for winning, and it was contagious. It really was."

Jerry Kramer
G, Green Bay Packers,
1961, 1962, 1965, 1966, 1967

"I was fortunate to win two Super Bowls in my career, but winning that first one, and being a part of that 17–0 undefeated season, that was certainly the most important achievement of my career. It's the only perfect season in the 90-year history of the NFL, so it's significant."

Bob Kuechenberg
OL, Miami Dolphins, 1972, 1973

"Complete and utter satisfaction, that's what it meant to me. It's a tremendous thrill to win a championship at any level and in any sport, but certainly winning the Super

Bowl is right up there in terms of prestige and reputation. As a football player, this is it, it's the pinnacle. Every team starts out the year with that same goal, to win the championship, and in the end there is only one team left standing. Fortunately, I was able to be on two different teams that were the last ones standing, and it means a lot. I came from a very small town, went to a small college, and was never even drafted. So the journey for me was a long one. I worked hard though and am very proud to be a champion in this league. Once you win it, they can never take it away from you. Winning the Super Bowl, it's forever."

Jim Langer
C, Miami Dolphins, 1972, 1973

"It was the fourth Super Bowl, and it was significant in the sense that it proved without a doubt that the AFL was every bit as good, if not better, than the NFL. The Jets had won the year before, and with that it was now 2–2; two wins for the NFL and two wins for the AFL. The two leagues would of course merge after that 1969 season, but it showed the sporting world that we were to be taken seriously. It's a unique struggle to get to the top, it really is. A lot of things have to come together for a team to reach the pinnacle as we did that year. Other than Len Dawson getting injured early in the season, we were all pretty healthy for the most part, and that was a big factor. We just all came together at the right time, and fortunately we were able to achieve our ultimate goal, to win the Super Bowl. Minnesota had a good team that year, but fortunately we were able to execute our game plan and come out on top."

Willie Lanier
LB, Kansas City Chiefs, 1969

"I was thrilled to win it in 1971–72 because we had lost to Baltimore the year before in Super Bowl V. Our goal from the first day of training camp was to win the Super Bowl; it was our singular mission. That was it. That was our goal, and we were determined to do it. Losing such a close game to Baltimore [16–13] really drove us. It left a very bad taste in our mouths. We were hungry, we were all business, and we weren't going to be denied. We were going 100 percent every day in practice, on a mission. We were mechanically strong and really worked on not making mistakes. Our attitude was overwhelmingly positive throughout the season, despite the fact that we started out slowly and were 4–3 midway through the season. We just kept working hard and got better and better each week. In fact, we didn't lose another game that season. We got a lot of momentum on our side midway through the year, and that carried us through the playoffs.

For me, personally, it had been a long time coming. We had come up short to Lombardi's Packers in the '66 and '67 title games and had gotten knocked out of the playoffs several other times. I was tired of hearing us referred to as 'next year's champions,' 'can't win the big one,' and the one that hurt the most: 'the bridesmaids of the NFL,' which was given to us by *Sports Illustrated.* So, to win it and to finally become a champion was just fantastic. After all those years of disappointment, I was ready to finally win the big one.

As for the game itself, it was a thrill. We beat Miami, 24–3, down in New Orleans at the old Sugar Bowl. They had a very, very good football team, but we were just so determined that day. I don't think there was anybody who could've beaten us. I really don't. The Dolphins would go on to win it the next year by going undefeated, so there was no question as to just how good they were. We had been preparing for that game, regardless of who it was going to be against, mentally and physically all year though—and this was *our* time.

Our guys were just not going to be denied. Several players on our squad had been hurt during the latter part of the season, but everybody played. That was why we prevailed—everybody was on board. Miami had a great running game with Larry Csonka and Jim Kiick, but our flex defense played superb, and we shut them down. We kept [quarterback Bob] Griese in check too, and that was no easy task. He was a heck of a football player.

Overall, it was just the ultimate team win. We never glorified our individuals, only the team. It was all about the team that year, and everybody bought into that. To hoist that trophy up was just absolutely fantastic. I will never forget how great it felt afterward, celebrating with all my teammates. We had a huge party that night and brought in [country music singer] Charley Pride—it was pretty special.

You know, I was the Cowboys' first draft choice ever, so I had seen it all up until that point...literally. We were a brand-new team in 1961, and we went through our share of growing pains. By the time we won it, there was very little luck involved—we had worked our butts off and paid our dues. Looking back, whenever I think about it I just have to smile. It was wonderful then, and it's wonderful today."

Bob Lilly
DT, Dallas Cowboys, 1971

"It was absolutely amazing. I'll never forget that moment when we won it for the rest of my life. Holding that trophy, that was the coolest. The best part about it for me was the fact that it was in my hometown, Minneapolis, that year. So I got to really enjoy it and share it with all of my friends and family. I felt the stress though, of being the hometown guy and having to deal with all the media and whatnot. That was tough, but I enjoyed it. I remember taking a bunch of my teammates out ice fishing on Prior Lake with some guys from ESPN—what a blast that was. A lot of the guys, especially the southerners, had never been on top of a frozen lake before. They were freaking out when we started driving out to our fish house, thinking for sure we were going under. They truly were 'fish out of water.' It was pretty hilarious.

The big bonus for me was the fact that I had played my college football at the University of Minnesota, and we played our home games at the Metrodome. So I felt extremely comfortable being in there. That gave me a lot of confidence, which, as a kicker, is a pretty big part of the game. Positive image and positive attitude, that's the key. My teammates believed in me, and I fed off of that. From a personal standpoint, I had a very successful season statistically. I led the league in scoring and had a lot of game-winning field goals too, so I was ready to go.

As for the game, we dominated Buffalo that day and won it 37–24. All of that hard work, from training camp on, it all came together that Sunday, and we were able to take care of business. Our goal from day one was to get there and win it, and we did it. So it was extremely gratifying. To hold that trophy with your teammates, what a feeling. It was humbling. Having grown up as a Vikings fan, and watching the team lose four Super Bowls, it makes you realize how many great players never get that opportunity to win it. I was just very fortunate to have been a part of such an amazing team."

Chip Lohmiller
K, Washington Redskins, 1991

"We went 1–11 my rookie year, and it took us a while to become winners. So when we won that iconic championship in 1958, 'The Perfect Game' against the Giants, it meant a great deal to me because of how far we had come. I actually broke my ankle at the end of that game. It hurt like heck, but I refused to go to the locker room. They asked me why not, and I told them that I had waited so long for that moment and that there was no way I was going to miss celebrating with my teammates out on the field if we won. Well, once we went into overtime, the coaches forced me to get out of there because they were worried that I would get trampled if the fans all stormed the field at Yankee Stadium. So, I wasn't out there for the celebration. We won it though, and I was very proud of that. We did it again that next year too, which was just an incredible experience because this time we got to do it at home in front of our own fans."

Gino Marchetti
DE, Baltimore Colts, 1958, 1959

"You start to play this kid's game as a kid, and you grow from a kid to a young man, and from a young man you become a grown man—still getting to play that same kid's game, only now for a king's ransom. The money was great, sure, but you don't play for the money—you play for the love of the game. So for a guy like me to be able to play this game I loved so dearly well into my thirties, and to win a pair of championships along the way, what a blessing. The only other thing in my life that made me feel greater in terms of achievement, other than winning those Super Bowls, was becoming a father."

Leonard Marshall
DE, New York Giants, 1986, 1990

"What a feeling. There's 32 teams out there all with the same goal. What separates you from all the others? The fact that we stayed resilient the whole year; we've been through a lot. We've been on the road throughout the entire playoffs, and we just stuck with our game plan. We've got a great cast and crew on this team, and what can you say? We're world champions, and nobody can take that away from us." [5]

Clay Matthews
LB, Green Bay Packers, 2010

"The name of the game in any sport is to win a championship. So, it's certainly the highlight of my 17-year career to be a part of a world championship team. I had lost a championship game earlier in my career, back in '58, when I was a rookie with the Giants and we lost to Baltimore in the 'Perfect Game.' So to win it with the Jets in '68, and beat those Colts again, that was pretty special. Just getting to the Super Bowl is an accomplishment in itself. The biggest game of my career was the AFL Championship Game where we beat the Oakland Raiders. That was the big one because you have to win that or there is no Super Bowl. That was the pressure game. In fact, I was very relaxed at the Super Bowl; heck, I enjoyed it. Why? Because just for showing up I knew that I was going to at least be getting the 'loser's share' bonus of $7,500. But, if we played a little harder, we could get the 'winner's share,' which was $15,000. Heck, I was a plumber in the off-season in those days, so that was quite an incentive. It was just a huge honor to be the first AFL team to win the Super Bowl. Green Bay had won the first two, and everybody just figured that the older, more established NFL was going to keep on winning them. Well, we put an end to that in a hurry. We used that as motivation. We felt disrespected by all of that talk and just focused on winning the game."

Don Maynard
WR, New York Jets, 1968

"To be a world champion, that's what you work for in this business. That was the pinnacle, the highest high. It was very gratifying, no question. To beat the New York Giants, who were always in contention in those days, it was just a wonderful experience. It's just something you will never forget."

Lenny Moore
RB, Baltimore Colts, 1958, 1959

"It meant everything to me. It's something I used to dream about as a kid, playing in the backyard with my neighborhood buddies. I would imagine myself scoring the game-winning touchdown. So, to live my dream come true, it's beyond words. It's pretty sweet. It was like God opened up the skies and allowed us to have a little piece of heaven on earth. I have a wonderful memory of me holding the Lombardi Trophy in one arm and my 18-month-old daughter in the other right after we beat Arizona. Whenever I look at that picture I just have to smile. How sweet is that?"

Mewelde Moore
RB, Pittsburgh Steelers, 2008

"It's the epitome of your profession to win the Super Bowl. To put all that time and preparation in and to ultimately be rewarded with a championship is extremely gratifying. That's what you go to training camp for. To see all your hard work and dedication come to fruition, that's just a very special feeling."

Tom Moore
Offensive Coordinator, Indianapolis Colts, 2006

"I have vivid memories of losing Super Bowl III when I was with the Colts, and we were upset by Joe Namath and the Jets. Johnny Unitas was injured in the final exhibition game that season, and I became the team's starter for the rest of the way. We went 13–1 but wound up getting upset in Super Bowl III. I was named as the MVP of the league that year, but I would have gladly given it back in a heartbeat to have won it. That was tough. Having that taste of success though, it drove me. I really wanted that championship. We wound up winning it two years later when we beat the Cowboys, 16–13, in Super Bowl V. What an amazing feeling that was, to be on top of the world. In Miami, we had the perfect combination of good players and good people who all worked together. We of course would go on to win Super Bowls VII and VIII, which included the undefeated perfect season of 1972. We had a great camaraderie together, which you don't always see on teams. So to be a part of three championship teams with the Colts and Dolphins, it meant a great deal. To be a champion, the best of the best, that's what it's all about. And yes, I still enjoy making the champagne toast along- side my '72 teammates every time the last undefeated team gets beat each year. Some people have commented that they don't think it's right that we cheer for them to lose, but that's not how we see it. We're just cheering for the other team to win. That's all. Hey, we earned that. And until somebody comes along and goes undefeated, well, we'll just keep on cheering!"

Earl Morrall
QB, Baltimore Colts, 1970;
Miami Dolphins, 1972, 1973

"That's what I'm most proud of in my career, those two world championships. It doesn't hit you right away, but later on when you can sit back and reflect on it, you real- ize that it was a pretty incredible accomplishment. To be a part of those two teams was something I will never forget. I had some outstanding teammates, I tell you what: Ray Berry and John Unitas to name a few. John was one cool customer. He didn't say a whole lot out there, but boy could he play. He was so tough. We would do just about anything for him, he was *our* guy. We only had 35 ballplayers on our team in those days, so we were close. We were like a family. Everybody got along, and we enjoyed socializing with each other outside of football too, after practices and during the off-season. We played together as a unit and stood up for each other out there. Our defense was so good in those days, just really top notch. In fact, we had 75 interceptions over those two sea- sons, which is still an NFL record. I had eight myself in '58 and really prided myself on forcing turnovers. Those are big momentum swingers, turnovers, and they give the offense a big boost. So, you don't hear much about that record, but it was certainly a big factor in our success those two seasons."

Andy Nelson
CB, Baltimore Colts, 1958, 1959

"The feeling is unbelievable. It encapsulates everything you worked your whole career for. It's the ultimate team championship. To win a championship at that level, I'll just never forget the feeling. I grew up dreaming of winning it, so when it finally happened for me it truly was a dream come true."

Stacy Robinson
WR, New York Giants, 1986, 1990

"Getting drafted by the San Francisco 49ers was such a blessing for me. I was immediately put into a situation where the culture was all about being the best. I remember shortly after arriving there [coach] Bill Walsh saying to us that our goal was to win a world championship and that nothing less was going to be acceptable to this organization. That was the stated goal from day one. Wow. I was so blown away. Well guess what? We went out and did exactly that, winning the Super Bowl in '89. Then, from the first day of training camp that next season, the goal was all about repeating. Sure enough, that was exactly what we did, winning it again in '90. My first two years in the league, and we were the two-time defending world champions. It was unbelievable. We were just so confident in our abilities as a team; we just knew that as long as we executed our game plans, that we were going to win. Of course the next year it was about a three-peat, and we were close, but we came up short against the Giants in the NFC Championship Game. We didn't get it done and were all devastated. We fell short of our expectations, and it hurt, all of us hurt. We simply did not want to let not only ourselves down, but we didn't want to let the organization down.

Playing in San Francisco was a totally unique experience for me. I get asked a lot about why they were so good in those days, and my answer is that they had a unique style all their own, which they used to refer to as the '49er Way.' The 49er Way was about being the best. Period. Whether that was in a meeting room, on the practice field, on the playing field, or on the team plane, it was just about being held to that standard. To me, it started at the very top with our owner, Eddie DeBartolo. He was *always* doing things right. It was the little things to him that made the biggest difference. The Niners organization had an aura about it in those days—guys wanted to play there. They wanted to play there not only because we were the best on the field, we were also the best off the field. They took care of their players and provided us with whatever we needed.

For instance, we had our *own* rooms on the road in hotels. That was huge. No roommates. Plus, we could watch free movies while we were in our rooms, stuff like that, little things that you might not think about—but they went a long way with us. When we traveled, we flew on a DC-10, not much smaller than a 727. For big guys like us, having all that extra leg room, it was awesome. You could relax and kick back. Plus, no layovers, just nonstops. Even the food on board was unbelievable, just first class all the way. I remember at Christmas, all of our wives, girlfriends, or significant others would get $500 gift certificates to

Neiman Marcus to go shopping. If you had a baby, there were a dozen roses sent to you from the 49er family. I remember after we won the Super Bowl in '90, Eddie flew all of us, spouses included, to Hawaii to celebrate. And what a bash that was. He paid for all the golf and food too—it was insane.

Even at training camp they treated us right. Every player dreads training camp, especially the first couple of weeks. You typically get worked to death at the two-a-day practices, and you basically just worked your ass off. Well, the Niners didn't do it that way. Coach Walsh didn't believe in killing us in training camp. In the first week he didn't even make us wear pads in the afternoon sessions, and eventually we would just do walk-throughs. It was amazing. He trusted us to get in shape and didn't want to wear us out. He wanted us to be fresh not only when the season started, but also come playoff time.

All of those little things, they added up. They made you *want* to win for him and for the organization. So when I was a young guy with the team, it was up to the older veterans, guys like Ronnie Lott, Joe Montana, Jerry Rice, Roger Craig, and Michael Carter, to make sure everybody did things the right way, that nobody screwed up. They policed us. They made sure we were accountable and were holding ourselves to those 49er Way standards. They made sure that when we were out there playing, it was all about perfection. Nothing less was acceptable. It wasn't just expected, it was demanded. As a result, that attitude and gratitude showed out on the field. Everybody was on the same mission and that was to win. Period. When you win, guys get higher salaries; coaches get job security; and owners get lots of money. Success fuels success, and that was the basis of it all.

*Bill Romanowski reacts in the closing seconds of the Denver Broncos'
Super Bowl XXXII win over the Green Bay Packers. Romanowski won
four Super Bowls, two each as a member of the San Francisco 49ers and
Broncos. (AP Images)*

Anyway, I went through a dry spell over the next seven years
where I was a part of three NFC Championship Game
losses. That was tough. Really tough. When you are used to
winning, losing absolutely sucks. I started to realize how special it was to be a Super Bowl champion. I also realized how
hard it was to achieve it. I realized just how much blood,

sweat, and tears actually go into making it a reality. You have to go through so much, starting at training camp and winding all the way through the season, but when you come out as the last guys standing—it's amazing. Just amazing. When you get to raise that trophy after you've won the Super Bowl, it's one of the most intense highs I've ever had in my life. So, I found myself chasing that high. That was my drug; I needed that championship. After I had been spoiled as a first- and second-year player, winning two in a row, I came back to earth in a big way. It wasn't completely about winning the title either; it was about being the absolute best, about what that meant, about being a part of a great team, and about how good that all felt.

So when I signed with Denver and we went out and beat Green Bay in '98, that was the Super Bowl that I appreciated the most. I was so hungry for it and had missed and craved it so much—it was incredible. We didn't win our division that year, so we had to do it on the road that post-season. We beat Jacksonville in the first round, the team that had beaten us the year before to end our season, and then Kansas City in the second round, and lastly we upset Pittsburgh in the AFC Championship Game. From there we had to take on the defending champion Packers, and we knew it was going to be tough. We were 13-point under-dogs in that game, but we knew we were better than they were. Our coach, Mike Shanahan, had set the bar of win-ning that championship in minicamp though, and we were so determined. He told us that nothing less than that ring was going to be acceptable to the organization, and that was exactly what I needed to hear. We just came out and played inspired football, and we did it. To accomplish that goal was so gratifying. To see John Elway finally get his ring, it gives me goose bumps just thinking about it. What a great group of guys; we were so tight. Collectively we really liked each other, which is rare in football. We all got along and had just great chemistry, both on and off the field. We came into training camp the next season and set that goal right there again, to win the championship, and sure enough—we did it again. Beating Atlanta that next year was special, but it wasn't anything like the feeling we had the year before. We were expected to win it this time, and we did. It was fantastic, don't get me wrong, but it was different in that we knew that we were *going* to do it from day one, and then we simply went out and did it.

I just feel very blessed to have been able to play this game and to have been a part of four pretty amazing Super Bowl–winning teams. When I think of all the guys who have played in this league over the years who haven't won it, it's pretty humbling. I don't take anything for granted though, no way. There was a lot of hard work that went into it, along with a little bit of luck, but in the end we were able to take care of our business and persevere. I'm just really proud to say I'm a champion because they can never take it away from you. Never."

Bill Romanowski

LB, San Francisco 49ers, 1988, 1989;
Denver Broncos, 1997, 1998

"It was something I'd always dreamt and fantasized about, so when it finally happened it was almost like a religious experience."

Alex Sandusky

G, Baltimore Colts, 1958, 1959

"It was the perfect season, what more could you ask for? It was, and still remains, the only perfect season in NFL history—so it's historic. We had lost in the Super Bowl the year before, in 1971, to the Dallas Cowboys, so we were hungry to redeem ourselves. We had a lot of close games that year, but somehow we were always able to find a way to get the job done. We won that year because we had a leader by the name of Don Shula. He was the difference that season in my opinion. We did it with a bunch of no-name defensive players and a handful of reject offensive linemen. We had a good football team that didn't know that they were great until after that season.

For me personally, in addition to being immensely gratifying, it also gave me the credibility and experience necessary to become an NFL head coach. Just two weeks after the season ended I accepted the top job of the Baltimore Colts. I know that being a part of that coaching staff and having worked with Don [Shula] played a big part in that too. Looking back, I am extremely proud to say that I was a member of that team. We had a heckuva run, and in some ways, it's never really ended. It was big for all of us; we all shared in it. Because it had never happened before it was obviously significant. We all sort of became immortalized. I know that a lot of the players from that team still have a toast whenever the last undefeated team loses its first game of the year; it's their tradition that they have been doing for nearly 40 years now. I don't do it physically, but mentally I am toasting a tall one right alongside of them. I thought it was all over a few years ago when New England came close, right up until the Super Bowl, but our undefeated season still remains intact."

Howard Schnellenberger
Assistant Coach, Miami Dolphins, 1972

"It meant a lot. It was a goal that we set out to accomplish from the beginning of that season, so to see it come to fruition was extremely satisfying. Coach Ditka came in with a vision and a plan, and fortunately we had the talent to execute it. We had such an outstanding team that year, we really did. We had a crazy, rambunctious group of guys, all types of different characters with all sort of different personalities. So, Coach Ditka was able to bring us all together and lead us to the ultimate prize, the Super Bowl. It was incredible, certainly the high point of my playing career."

Mike Singletary
LB, Chicago Bears, 1985

"It means a lot because once you become a Super Bowl champion, they can never take that away from you. That ring is yours for life. Getting to the Super Bowl isn't enough; you have to get there and win it. There are a lot of great players who have gotten there, but only the winners are champions. So, I'm very proud of the fact that I'm a champion. When I go around and speak to groups and to young people, I tell them to make sure that they're winners, not losers. Everybody loves a winner and nobody loves a loser."

Otis Sistrunk
DE, Oakland Raiders, 1976

"What did it mean? I've played in two Super Bowls over the past four years. I've won one and I've lost one, so I've seen both sides. Trust me when I tell you that it's a heck of a lot better winning it than it is losing it. Winning it? It's just totally surreal. It takes a long, long time for it to set in— to realize just how special it really is. When you think about how many guys have played in this league over the years who have never gotten that opportunity, so many great players, it's very humbling. To know that you will always be remembered as a member of a championship team, the greatest team in the world that season, that's significant, it really is."

Matt Spaeth
TE, Pittsburgh Steelers, 2008

"It meant everything because that's obviously your ultimate objective as a player. You must take into consideration when you are building something that it's all about team—and I'm going to spell it out because I don't think enough people understand just what that word stands for. T) together E) everyone A) achieves M) more. People need to understand what the strength of that word is. You cannot do it any other way in my opinion. That's what championships are all about; they're all about the team. We were just so grateful to be in Green Bay and to have won it for those amazing fans. I'm obviously very biased, but I firmly believe that those are the greatest fans in the world. We were privileged to train, practice, and play in front of those people. You came to appreciate the genuineness of them, their unique loyalty, and their fanaticism of being Packer fans."

Bart Starr
QB, Green Bay Packers,
1961, 1962, 1965, 1966, 1967

"For me to win it in my first year in the league, against the team I grew up rooting for—the Vikings—it was beyond words. What an exciting time that was. Looking back, it's all just a blur. I was only 21 years old, a rookie fresh out of the University of Minnesota, and here I was playing in the biggest game of the year against the vaunted 'Purple People Eaters.' Everybody thought we were going to get slaughtered, and nobody was giving us a chance.

The Super Bowl in 1969–70 hadn't become the extravaganza it is today, but it was still a pretty big deal. The thing I remember most about that game was the enormous expectations going in. The fans in Kansas City were still so upset about the Chiefs losing Super Bowl I to Green Bay, three seasons earlier, and they wanted redemption. We could feel the pressure from the fans, from the media, from the coaches, and from the older veterans who wanted to finally beat those you-know-whats from the hated NFL. I remember the entire community was tuned in to the game. There was even a report that at halftime a major water line had burst in Kansas City due to the fact that everybody had gotten up to use the bathroom, and apparently the system was not equipped to handle all of those people flushing their toilets at the same time. The fans lived and died with the Chiefs, and they wanted a winner. It's a great football town, just fantastic.

Anyway, the rivalry in those days between the two leagues was just enormous. The Jets had won it the year before, but most felt like it was a 'Joe Namath fluke.' You see, Super Bowl IV, this was the last year before the NFL and AFL would completely merge into one league. Today we know them as the AFC and NFC, but in those days they were two completely separate rival leagues who had been competing viciously for players for a long, long time. There was a lot of bad blood there. The AFL, of which the Chiefs were members, felt completely disrespected by the NFL, and we wanted to beat them badly. The NFL had been around for much longer, and they viewed us as inferior. They referred to us as a Mickey Mouse league and said that most of our guys weren't even good enough to play in the NFL. Well, as you can imagine, that just infuriated us. It was ridiculous, of course, because most of the players had been drafted by the NFL but had signed with the AFL in order to make more money or to garner more playing time. We had seven future NFL Hall of Fame players on our roster, so it was a preposterous statement that was said to just add fuel to the fire I suppose.

I will never forget going into the locker room to get ready for our game against Minnesota. We immediately noticed that our coach, Hank Stram, had patches of the AFL logo sewn onto the sleeves of our jerseys. It was a big deal. We didn't have special jerseys or anything like that in those days; we pretty much wore the same one for the entire season. Well, to see it all cleaned up with this big beautiful patch on it was something else. It meant so much to some of the older guys, the veterans who had been around for the entire decade of the AFL's existence, that they literally started to cry when they saw this. It was a big psychological advantage for us.

Just the road to get there was so tough. We were a wild-card and had to go on the road. First we had to beat the Jets, who had just won the Super Bowl the year before and then we had to get past Oakland, who had beaten us twice. That was no picnic. Then it was the Minnesota Vikings, who were just a fantastic team. We beat them pretty handily, 23–7, and made history in the process. We just had a great defense and wound up giving up a total of 20 points in all three games. It was unbelievable, it really was. So, looking back, I don't know if I truly appreciated what I had been a part of at the time, but certainly winning the Super Bowl has become much more impactful as the years have gone by.

For me personally, it was a thrilling yet frustrating season. I was a rookie linebacker playing behind Willie Lanier and Bobby Bell, both Hall of Famers. Hank [Stram] was the kind of coach too in that he played the best guys. Period. So, I played special teams and did what I could, basically just paying my dues until I could earn more playing time as I got more experience. I remember recovering a key fumble late in the game against the Jets in the playoffs that year, and it iced the game for us. To do that against the defending Super Bowl champs, that was the highlight of the year for me. I will never forget my teammates congratulating me out on the field—it was amazing. Just to feel like I was contributing was such a big boost to my ego. I wish I had many more memories like that about the '69 season, but I knew that I had to just sit tight and not rock the boat. Hey, no complaints though. I was happy as could be to be on a Super Bowl–winning team in my first year in the league. I just wish I could have won a whole bunch more."

Bob Stein

LB, Kansas City Chiefs, 1969

"This was the last ever game between the AFL and the NFL, so it was historic. We, as the representatives of the AFL, were deemed as the league that was not as good as the NFL. So for us, we had all sorts of extra motivation to win. We wanted to show the world that we were not only as good as the older, more established NFL; we wanted to prove that we were better. And we did. The Chiefs had lost in Super Bowl I to Green Bay a few years earlier, pretty badly at 35–10, so the satisfaction of beating

Minnesota pretty handily that day was enormous. We were 14-point underdogs coming into the game and wound up winning 23–7. We had a dominating defense and just shut them down. The Vikings had a great, great football team that season, but I think we had extra incentive to win that day. We had worked so hard, practiced so hard, sacrificed so much, gone through so much adversity, and now we were the world champions. What a feeling. The joy of winning a team championship, versus an individual championship, is the fact that you can share the exuberance with your teammates as well as with your fans. I think the only people in America who thought we could beat Minnesota that day were us, the Chiefs, and thank God we did!

As for the game itself, I remember the conditions that day were nothing to write home about, trust me. It was down in New Orleans at old Tulane Stadium. The field was a mess. It looked nothing like the fields we have today, which look like pristine putting greens. It was a blustery, cold day. There were even tornado warnings earlier in the day. The tarp that covered the field had several tears in it, and there were some big mud holes out on the field—it was bad. I remember two out of the three field goals I made that day were right in some very slippery, muddy spots. Fortunately though, I was able to get a decent footing and put them all through the uprights and help my team win that day. The wind was a factor too. Minnesota had the first opportunity to score on a 50-yard field goal but opted to punt instead. So, I was able to put us up 9–0 on three early kicks, and that really got the momentum going in our favor. As a kicker, you want to get involved early and get your confidence up, that was a big factor. I was young, excited, full of adrenaline—I think I could have kicked one from 60 yards that day. Some days you have it and others you don't. Well, I had it that day."

Jan Stenerud

K, Kansas City Chiefs, 1969

"It was just a really good feeling knowing that you were a world champion. I was very fortunate to have been able to accomplish that goal as a member of four different Packer teams. So, to know that you were a member of a team that was the best of the best that particular season, it's a fabulous legacy to be a part of. I am often asked about why those teams were so good, and my answer always starts with the fact that we were blessed to have the best coach in football in those days, Vince Lombardi. His leadership and conviction for what he believed in were so strong. Beyond that, we had 10 Hall of Fame players on those teams during the '60s, so we had some outstanding talent. Yes, I had some great, great teammates.

For me it was just all about the team; everything was about helping my teammates to strive to be the best we could be. Whether it was putting my head down and punishing that would-be tackler along the sideline with a big hit or working hard to protect the football, I was always thinking about how my actions were going to affect my teammates. You know, I rarely ever fumbled the ball. Turnovers were momentum killers, and I just did not want to let down my teammates, so I always tried as hard as I could to hold on to the ball. I was the type of player where I wanted the ball all the time. I wanted it in my hands so that I could do something good with it to help my teammates. That was my mentality. I wanted to do whatever I could to help us win, and win big. In football and in life, it comes down to those little things. Little things like that I think are what makes good teams great, and we had some great, great teams in those days. I was just very proud to be a member of so many of those outstanding Green Bay Packer teams."

Jim Taylor
RB, Green Bay Packers,
1961, 1962, 1965, 1966

"What did it mean to raise Lombardi? It's almost indescribable. You're at a loss for words when it happens because it's such a profound moment. Your whole world changes in an instant. Really, it's been a whole new world for me since I was able to raise it 28 years ago. All sorts of new doors open when you become a champion. It makes a big difference. The history, the tradition, it's all a part of it. And when it all comes together, there's just a great sense of pride that goes along with it."

Joe Theismann
QB, Washington Redskins, 1982

"It was the fulfillment of a seemingly unreachable goal. As a kid, dreaming of being a professional athlete is always there, but to dream of being a Super Bowl champion? That's almost untouchable, unreachable, hardly a realistic option. So for me to actually win it was a pretty surreal experience. It was certainly a product of a lot of hard work, but there was obviously an element of luck and timing too. I was just very fortunate to have been able to be a part of such an amazing team. The stars aligned for me, and I'm very grateful. Hey, truth be told, I grew up as a hockey goalie, and my big dream as a kid was to hoist the Stanley Cup. So to win the Super Bowl wasn't even on my radar as a kid. And while there weren't many recruiters interested in six-foot-seven goalies, they were interested in six-foot-seven tight ends—so everything just kind of worked out for me.

It was a very special time for a lot of reasons. First, it's the fulfillment of a lot of personal goals that were reached. Second, it's special for your family who has always stood by you throughout your entire career. Third, for me personally, I felt very proud to be from the state of Minnesota. I am a loyalist, that was why I stayed at home for college, and when I won it, I felt a big sense of pride for my home state. It was special because I was able to bring a piece of the Lombardi Trophy back home, which is something very few native Minnesotans have been able to do over the years."

Ben Utecht
TE, Indianapolis Colts, 2006

"What a feeling. To win it, what a feeling. You know, you start out every season thinking and hoping that this could be the year. You think, *We can do it!* You give it your all, you try like hell, but then as the season goes on you deal with all the injuries and you're tired and you're beat up, and a million different things go wrong along the way. The dream never fades away, but you realize at a certain point that it's not going to happen that season. Then the next season comes and you get close, but you come up short. Then you start thinking about just how many more chances you're going to get at it, because your body can only go for so long in this league. I played 13 years in the league and had been to the playoffs 10 times. Every year was the same. The closer you would get, the more you would feel like it was never going to happen. Then, finally, after going through so much, you get that chance, and you win it. It's just the greatest feeling in the world. It was such an odd feeling because you're almost like a robot, just programmed to not win it and to be able to accept that horrible feeling after every season. So to win it is so validating, so rewarding. You finally get to feel good about yourself and about your teammates. It's so hard to describe, the feeling. I can't explain it, really. To finally be able to enjoy that long off-season? That was it. What a feeling. I'm not even sure I really even fully enjoyed it until 10–15 years after I was retired. Then all of a sudden you start realizing, 'Man, you did something that was very, very difficult to do.' Then you look around and you see a Vince Lombardi Trophy in your house and a Super Bowl ring, and then you realize that you are one of the elite who were able to do that. So it's very difficult to enjoy it when you win it, but it stays with you for the rest of your life. The staying power and the uniqueness of being in that club, that's the most exciting thing to me."

Phil Villapiano
LB, Oakland Raiders, 1976

"From a football standpoint, it's the ultimate. Winning a team championship at that level is the ultimate goal as a player, and I was just very fortunate to have been a member of some really outstanding teams in Pittsburgh that were able to get the job done. Winning a championship takes a while to sink in though. At the time it happens you are so excited and exhausted, so you can't really appreciate it. Later on when you sit back and reflect upon the achievement, you realize just how special and significant it really is. Some of those teams that I was a part of are still considered to be among the very best of all time, and that means a lot as well. My family is from Wisconsin and I grew up as a Packer fan, so to hoist the Lombardi Trophy has an even extra meaning to me."

Mike Wagner
S, Pittsburgh Steelers,
1974, 1975, 1978, 1979

"Anytime you can do something where it means you are at the peak of your career, the pinnacle, it's an amazing accomplishment. That's what winning the Super Bowl means. Hoisting that trophy at the end of the season means one thing, success. It means you're a champion."

Mike Walter
LB, San Francisco 49ers,
1984, 1988, 1989

"It was probably the most exciting moment of my life, to walk off the field as a champion. In fact, I can remember as I was leaving the field, with nearly 80,000 of our fans cheering us on, looking up at the light poles and thinking how amazing it would be to climb up there and scream at the top of my lungs, 'I'm a world champion!' The joy of being the best of the best was almost indescribable. When you win it, that crescendo probably only lasts 15 minutes, but the satisfaction that it evokes lasts a lifetime. What was so special about it was the fact that it was a total team effort. We won together as a team. It didn't matter how big your role was; it didn't matter where you came from; it didn't matter what color you were—we were a group of people who genuinely cared about one another. So, it meant everything to me."

Paul Wiggin
DE, Cleveland Browns, 1964

"As a football player, your ultimate goal is to win the Super Bowl. So when it happened for me it was a dream come true. I had literally dreamed of winning the Super Bowl as a kid. It was amazing. I grew up in Pittsburgh as a huge Steelers fan and have so many great memories of them winning all those Super Bowls back in the '70s. Add to that the fact that my dad was an All-American quarterback at Notre Dame, and it's pretty obvious as to why I love the game of football so much. I grew up around it and was immersed into it from an early age.

As for the game itself, it was just a huge sense of relief when it was all said and done. What I mean by that is that it was actually more exciting beating San Francisco in the NFC Championship Game than it was beating Buffalo in the Super Bowl. When we beat the Niners, it was a thrill; we were going to the big game. There was such a joy shared by my teammates. Then, when we beat the Bills in such dramatic fashion, on the last play of the game, and had that tremendous weight lifted off of your shoulders—you were just relieved. You did it. You had reached the pinnacle. The journey was over. Now you could come up for air, relax, and reflect.

So many memories. I remember standing next to Whitney Houston during the National Anthem, wow, I just got goose bumps thinking about it. I remember the F-16s flying over the stadium in Tampa. I remember standing on the sideline at the end of the game thinking, *I can't believe we're going to lose the Super Bowl on a stupid field goal.* Then, to see that kick sail wide right, it was just the most beautiful thing. It was surreal. You couldn't help but feel bad for the kicker [Scott Norwood], but that's football. I was so excited; all I cared about was celebrating with my teammates and enjoying the moment.

Then, one of the downsides of us winning the Super Bowl in 1991 was the fact that because the Gulf War was going on, and security was so high, we never got to have a ticker-tape parade, and we never got to meet the president either. That was really a bummer, no doubt about it. We were thrilled to be champions, but that stuff would have been nice. The parade, certainly, for our fans; and to meet the president, selfishly, for myself. The heightened sense of security at the game was insane. I remember seeing armed soldiers with M-16s hanging around. I remember having FBI agents tear down our video equipment to make sure it all checked out. It was crazy.

My last memory came after the game, out in the parking lot. You see, my wife drove down from Minnesota in a huge RV with about 25 friends and family. So, we were all celebrating in it afterward, just out of our minds crazy, and in the midst of it all we realized that parked right next to us, in the very next stall, was [Buffalo quarterback] Jim Kelly. I just looked over at him and saw the look on his face. That look of despair on the poor man's face, it was brutal. It was at that moment where it hit me: there's a winner and there's a loser. I felt for him, I really did. I wanted to crawl under a rock at that point, but I obviously had nowhere to go.

I eventually got out of there and headed back to our team hotel. When I got there, all of the guys had set up an impromptu party out in the parking lot. It was a blowout, it was huge. All the old-timers were there, everybody just cut loose. We wound up blowing off a bunch of fireworks and just partying all night long—it was a moment I will never forget. It was at that moment I could finally just relax and enjoy the fruits of my labor. It was an incredible season, it really was."

Brian Williams
OL, New York Giants, 1990

"Winning the Super Bowl was amazing, and I had the privilege to be a part of three championship teams. For me, personally, the '95 Super Bowl was probably the most meaningful in that I was a starter. Each was special in its own way though, and each had its own unique journey. Looking back, sometimes it's not the games you won that you remember most, it's the ones you lost. You hate to look back at the negatives, but sometimes you do remember the interceptions over the touchdowns. When I think about all the Super Bowls we didn't win, because we never got there in the first place, that's so tough. We lost some really close NFC Championship Games during those years, and those were all squandered opportunities. We had some unbelievably talented teams back then, and quite frankly, we should have won even more than we did. We were just that good in my opinion.

There's nothing like being in the locker room right after you've won it and looking around and seeing that there are 50 other guys that did this with you. Seeing the joy in their eyes knowing that they're world champions, it's incredible. Just incredible. That feeling, personally, is like none other. The journey is *not* in winning the Super Bowl though. There have been so many great players who have had great careers, very fulfilling careers, but haven't been able to win it because they just didn't get the opportunity. This is a team game, and it takes the entire team to get there and to get the job done. So, yes, championships matter, and they should matter. But they shouldn't define you. I am very fortunate in that I have been able to win a few of them, but at the same time I feel for guys who, for whatever the reason, just didn't get that experience. I think that winning the Super Bowl defines you with the public more than anything. It creates an emotional cementing between fans and players that never gets taken away. You can have great seasons statistically, and you can do great things as a team, but over time the fans are really connected to you by championships. In that regard, being a champion is extremely meaningful and gratifying."

Steve Young
QB, San Francisco 49ers,
1988, 1989, 1994

Championship Teams

Whenever a team wins a championship, there are countless reasons why. I wanted to know why certain teams were able to win while others simply came up short. I wanted players to get specific, and I wanted them to get into the details of what made that team so unique. I wanted to know about that team's chemistry; about its leaders; about its motivation. I wanted to know which players played which roles and why. I wanted to better understand what the team did differently that season, compared to all the others, starting at training camp and going right up through the playoffs. Eventually, trends and patterns developed from the responses. Before long, you could see that winning teams, championship teams, had a different DNA. They were absolutely rare, and that was what made them so special.

WHY DID THAT CHAMPIONSHIP TEAM WIN?

"Perseverance. We all just pulled together and played through whatever we had to play through. I had a really bad calf injury early on that season that was just brutal. At times I could barely walk, and I don't think it got better until about Week 6 or 7. I finally started to come around after that but still felt kind of hobbled for the rest of the season. You're never really 100 percent healthy when you play this game, but you learn to play through it—that's just what you have to do. While I was injured though, I kind of became a coach on the sideline. I sort of mentored Willie Parker for the first part of that season, and it was very gratifying. Our team needed him to step up, despite him being so young and inexperienced, so I took it upon myself to work with him and do whatever I could to help him out and get him prepared. I knew that this was my last season and that my days were limited, so I wasn't necessarily worried about him taking my job. I was never insecure of situations like that. I was past all of that. I had always welcomed the competition throughout my career and just wanted to do what was best for the team. I wanted a ring and I knew that we needed him to be successful in order for that to happen. Luckily he came through and really played big for us."

Jerome Bettis
RB, Pittsburgh Steelers, 2005

"It started in the locker room. The chemistry with this team is great; guys like each other and we all get along. The character of the people who are on this team is amazing. I'd been with the team for four years prior to winning the Super Bowl, but this year was special. We added a few key people, and everything just came together for us. Guys really stepped up this year too. We had so many injuries to so many key people, yet guys responded and really came through for us. It was just a total team effort. You know, we had one goal this year and that was to win the championship, and I'm just so excited and proud of the fact that we were able to do that."

Mason Crosby
K, Green Bay Packers, 2010

Jerome Bettis celebrates with the Vince Lombardi Trophy after the Pittsburgh Steelers defeated the Seattle Seahawks in Super Bowl XL. The game was Bettis' last as an active player. (Jonathan Ferrey/Getty Images)

"I was fortunate to have been a part of two championship teams. The first one, 1981, we beat the Bengals, 26–21, in Detroit. Prior to that season, we were a group of guys who had achieved very little success. We were so young and dumb; we really didn't realize what we were doing until we had accomplished it. We certainly didn't expect to have that kind of success, that was for sure. One of the defining moments that season was when we beat Dallas pretty soundly, and afterward we realized that hey, we were actually pretty good. That gave us a lot of confidence and momentum, which carried us through the rest of the season and into the playoffs.

The second one came three years later in 1985 when we beat Miami, 38–16. We played this one at Stanford, which was great because it was sort of like a home game for us. This was a very different experience; it had a much different feeling to it. We were sort of expected to win this one, whereas the first one we sort of came out of nowhere. We were widely regarded as the best team in the league that year, so we felt the pressure this go around. We only lost one game that season; we had just an awesome team.

The Niners were a very unique organization in those days. Everybody wanted to play for the Niners in the '80s and '90s because they had a certain cache about them. For instance, we always flew to our away games in private chartered DC-10s. They were huge, and they had tons of leg room in there for us, which was really nice. Well, contrast that to the San Diego Chargers, who used to fly in much smaller 727s and then have to transfer to other planes in places like Oklahoma City. Our owner, Eddie DeBartolo, spared no expense on us. Everything was first class. We had gourmet catered food brought on board, we didn't have to wear suits, and we were really pampered.

Little stuff like that went a long way with a bunch of huge football players, trust me. Well, in return, we were expected to perform in that same manner of excellence on the field—we were expected to be the best. That was a big part of the whole equation as to why the organization was so successful year in and year out in those days."

Keith Fahnhorst
OT, San Francisco 49ers, 1981, 1984

"In my mind, it all started with Coach Ditka. He set the tone right out of the gates. He was just a breath of fresh air when it came to his leadership style. We had so many personalities on that team, and I think he was able to keep us all focused and on task. That was no easy task, but he did it. He had a very different approach to coaching, a very in-your-face attitude. He was going to play the best players too; he didn't care about all the politics and all of that other stuff. We had some great players on our roster that year. Every team in the National Football League has great players though, so what set this team apart from all the others was the fact that we had some outstanding leadership. Beyond that, we had a great team from top to bottom. Our defense that year was arguably one of the best in the history of the game, and I take great pride in that. We were so dominant that we could actually win games on defense—there were times when we outscored our offense. We were that good. After a while we had so much bravado and confidence, we just knew we had something special that season."

Leslie Frazier
CB, Chicago Bears, 1985;
Assistant Coach, Indianapolis Colts, 2006

"I have always believed that defense wins championships, whereas offense sells tickets. Don't get me wrong, we had a very good offense that season, but our defense was just outstanding. Our front four and linebackers especially, they were really good. Another reason why we won I believe is because we had the best kicker in football that year, Jan Stenerud. He was the difference in several games for us that season. He was just unbelievable. Or how about Len Dawson, our quarterback, he played fantastic as well. We had a great offensive line too; I can't forget about those guys. We just had a great team from top to bottom, that's why we won. We had great players and great coaches, and we all came together that season. That was *our* year. We had lost three years prior in the first Super Bowl, so we were very hungry this time around too. We vowed to get back, but it took us three more years of maturing as a team before we were able to do so. We all knew what it felt like to lose, and we were a lot less selfish this time in that everybody was willing to take on a role, even a lesser role, in order for the team to succeed. For instance, we had a backfield by committee, which no running back is ever thrilled about, but nobody complained. Everybody bought in, and that was why we had success that season."

Mike Garrett
RB, Kansas City Chiefs, 1969

"I think losing in the Super Bowl the year before [1971], to Baltimore, really made us hungry. That year our goal was to make it to the Super Bowl. Well, the following year our goal was to win it. Our focus had changed, from training camp on, and we were determined to get it done. We talked about it before every game, about how we were going to win the Super Bowl. It was our team focus, without a doubt. There were no individual goals for anyone that year—it was all about the team winning that championship. Then, once we got there, beating Miami became our obsession. They were the only thing standing between us and achieving that goal we had set at the beginning of the season. We started out strong and finished strong, winning 24–3. Roger [Staubach, quarterback] played a great game, and our defense was so tough. That was probably the most perfect game that I had ever been a part of. Other than Calvin Hill's fumble on the 2-yard line, which cost us another touchdown, it was nearly flawless. They had an outstanding team that year too, but we were just so determined. I don't think anybody was going to beat us to tell you the truth. We had some great, great players on that team."

Walt Garrison
RB, Dallas Cowboys, 1971

"That was our first year in Yankee Stadium, and it was a big deal for us. We had been playing over in the Polo Grounds and were sort of second-class citizens prior to that. That place was a dump, whereas Yankee Stadium was a palace. Anyway, this was our breakout year. We had finished third the year before, and everything just came together for us. We had quite a coaching staff. Our head coach was Jim Lee Howell, who actually didn't know very much about coaching, but he was an old Marine captain and ran a tight ship. So while he was out there blowing his whistle, his two coordinators were running the show, and they were pretty good. In fact, our offensive coordinator was Vince Lombardi, and our defensive coordinator was Tom Landry—both future Hall of Famers. Landry was actually a player-coach, so he was doing double duty for us.

We had a solid season. We had some great players too, guys like Rosey Grier, Sam Huff, Andy Robustelli, Emlen Tunnell, and of course our quarterback, Charlie Conerly. We got hot late in the year and wound up beating the Chicago Bears for the championship, 47–7. I remember Mel Triplett scoring. Alex Webster had a couple of touchdowns, Rick Casares got one [for the Bears], and so did Kyle Rote. I even got into the action late in the game when I scored on a 14-yard touchdown from Charlie Conerly. It was a thrill, it really was. We really beat up on those guys that day; everything was just clicking for us. Everything came together for us that season, and nobody got hurt too badly, which was always a big deal when you only had a 35-man roster. If guys got hurt, you were in trouble. I actually played a lot of defense, going both ways. That's how it was in those days. The game was at Yankee Stadium, and it was packed. The fans really got behind us that season and that was great to see.

Pro football was growing in status, and it's very humbling to think that our team was a part of that early growth. Early on I would say that our team was last in terms of popularity compared to the Yankees, Rangers, and Knicks, but after that win, that put us right up there with the Bronx Bombers. The Yankees were no longer the only show in town. Television was the key. Pro football was perfect theater for TV, and with the advent of television in the late '50s and into the '60s, so grew the game's popularity until it exploded in the '70s. Today, of course, it's a multibillion dollar empire, so to think back to the game's early beginnings and see how far it's come is pretty incredible."

Frank Gifford
HB, New York Giants, 1956

"I was fortunate in that I was able to win back-to-back Super Bowls with the Packers. The 1966 season was pretty special. We were pretty much the best team in the league all the way through the year, and we capped it by beating the Chiefs in the Super Bowl, 35–10. The next year might have been even more special though because of how we got there. I'm referring of course to the 'Ice Bowl,' where we beat Dallas up in Green Bay, 21–17. It was a rematch of the 1966 NFL title game, and there was no love lost between these two teams. Lombardi really wanted to beat these guys, and this game would go down in history. For starters, it was just about as miserable as you can imagine that day. It was so cold, something like 50-below wind chill, just horrible. The high school band couldn't even play at halftime because the kids' lips would get frozen to their instruments. I remember all the fans who were trying to get medical attention after the game because they had frostbite so bad. It came down to a simple will to win, I think, and the fact that our guys refused to lose. That last drive was something I will never forget. The field was just terrible; you couldn't get any footing out there whatsoever. It was frozen solid because the heating system that Lombardi had put in didn't work at all. It was tough. We were rewarded with a trip to Miami after that though, where we beat Oakland in the Super Bowl to make it two in a row. Those were great, great memories. Just wonderful."

Gale Gillingham
G, Green Bay Packers, 1966, 1967

"Just to get past Dallas in the title game, the 'Ice Bowl,' that was something else. What a game. It was beyond cold, and the footing was horrible. You could hardly stand up. We fought and fought and wound up on top. Boy, those guys were tough. Somehow we did it. But to win the first one, Super Bowl I, that was significant. It was the first time that the NFL and the AFL ever played each other. Going into that game it was the great unknown. Coach Lombardi had always prepared us well for our opposition, but this was totally different. We watched a lot of game film of the Kansas City Chiefs, but we simply didn't know how good the caliber of competition was at the time. I don't say that to be disrespectful of the other AFL teams who they played; I say it because we had never played against any of them and had no idea how good they really were. It made us all terribly nervous. We knew that they had some tremendous ballplayers over there though, some fantastic athletes, many of them would be Hall of Famers. There was just a great unknown going into the game, for both teams. We were representing the NFL, the older, established league. They were the new guys on the block, hungry and eager to prove that they were every bit as good as we were. It was a pretty exciting time to be a football fan at that time, because we were about to make history. It was something else. We felt the pressure, that was for sure. Well, we wound up beating them pretty good that day, 35–10, out in Los Angeles, and it was a huge relief. They had a very good football team, but I think we were just determined to win that game, no matter what. The pressure was on, and Vince really had us prepared to win. He kept reminding us that we were representing the NFL, and that hit home with us. We did *not* want to disappoint him. It was a wonderful feeling to win that first Super Bowl and to be a part of history. It was a moment I will certainly never forget."

Forrest Gregg

OT, Green Bay Packers,
1961, 1962, 1965, 1966, 1967

"Winning that first championship in '75 was a really big deal. Pittsburgh had never won it before, and we were so hungry. We went through a lot of adversity that season. I remember that was a strike year, and we missed a lot of training camp. We had some great talent coming in though, and that was a big boost for us. I think back to the draft we had that year. Our first four picks were Lynn Swann, Jack Lambert, John Stallworth, and Mike Webster. All of them are in the Hall of Fame; how incredible is that? So, we were a good football team before that, and we became a great football team after that. From there we had quarterback issues; it wasn't Terry Bradshaw all the way through. We had a couple guys starting games for us under center early on, and we struggled. We figured out that we were a running team about midway through the year, and I think that kind of put us in a groove. We had a great defense, so if we could just move the ball and get the lead, we knew that we would win some games.

We got on a roll late and our confidence soared. Bradshaw really came into his own during the latter part of the season, and it carried over into the playoffs. We beat Buffalo in the first playoff game but then had to go on the road to take on a very tough Oakland team in the AFC Championship Game. We were big rivals, and there was no love lost there between us. Winning on the road was huge for us. We were down 10–3 in the third quarter and then just turned it on. Franco Harris scored a couple of touchdowns in the fourth, and we hung on to win, 24–13. From there we met the Vikings in Super Bowl IX. Franco scored early in this one, and we never looked back. They were a really good team though, such a great defense, so it was a huge win for us. It was a pretty amazing feeling, to be a world champion, to be the best of the best. I'll never forget that first one; it was something else.

We repeated in '76, and it was extremely gratifying.
Whereas some people thought we came out of nowhere
and snuck up on some people the year before, winning it
again sort of validated us. It proved that we were no
fluke, that we were indeed for real. It was a real statement
for us to set out from day one with that goal of repeating
as world champions and then going out and actually
doing it. We went 12–2 that season and were really in
control from the beginning. We beat Baltimore and
Oakland in the playoffs and then got past the Cowboys in
the Super Bowl, 21–17. We were down early in this one
when Drew Pearson put Dallas up in the first, but we rallied back to tie it up. I think the big momentum swinger
came in the fourth quarter when we got a big safety, and
then Lynn Swann scored on a long touchdown pass from
Bradshaw to seal it.

We went through a rough patch over the next couple of
years. Oakland knocked us off in the conference championship the following season, and then we got beat by
Denver the year after that in the first round. We came into
our own in '78 though and established ourselves as a
passing team. Bradshaw really had great chemistry with
Lynn Swann, John Stallworth, and Jimmy Smith. We threw
the ball a lot more in those days and were putting up
higher numbers on the scoreboard. Our defense was still
very good, but certainly not as dominant as it was in the
first two Super Bowls. We were more balanced now, which
was good. We started out 7–0 and finished 14–2 that
year. We rolled over Denver and Houston in the playoffs
by big margins and then beat a very talented Dallas
Cowboys team in the Super Bowl, 35–31, down in Miami.
They were the defending champs, and we really wanted to
beat those guys. I remember John Stallworth scoring a

Steelers linebacker Jack Ham arranges the defense during Super Bowl X. Pittsburgh defeated the Dallas Cowboys 21–17, one of four Super Bowl wins for Ham's Steelers teams. (AP Images)

couple of touchdowns in this one; Rocky Bleier got one, Franco Harris got one, and Lynn Swann got one late. Bradshaw played really well, and we just hung on at the end. They scored twice late to make it interesting, but our defense came through for us. It was very meaningful to be back on top. We all appreciated it a little bit more this time because we had come up short the previous two tries, so that really lit the fire for us for the next year too.

The '79 team was our last hurrah. I actually didn't even get to play in this one because I had gotten hurt toward the end of the season. We were literally hanging on by this point, but we were able to somehow pull it together for one last shot. We beat the Rams in this one, and what made it so interesting was the fact that several of their coaches were former Steelers coaches under Chuck Noll. So, they knew what to expect from us, which forced us to really change up our game plan. The game was in Pasadena too, which was almost a home game for them. They were actually ahead at the half, 13–10, but we rallied behind a couple of long touchdown passes from Bradshaw to Lynn Swann and John Stallworth to pull ahead. We wound up winning the game, 31–19. We knew afterward that our run was over—everybody just knew. We were older and beat up and our time had passed. We were long in the tooth, especially on the defensive side of the ball. It was a heckuva run though, no doubt about it—one of the greatest in NFL history."

Jack Ham
LB, Pittsburgh Steelers,
1974, 1975, 1978, 1979

"I think it all starts with confidence. We knew that we had
a great team that year. We felt it; we believed it; we had
all the intangibles that are necessary to go all the way. My
story with that team was pretty unique. I came to the
Raiders from New England late in the season and was
billed as the 'missing piece of the puzzle,' which put a lot
of pressure on me. Several players told me that prior to me
coming they felt like they were going to get to the Super
Bowl, but then when I got there, they *knew* that they were
going to get to the Super Bowl—and win. They already
had a great team that year with some pretty awesome
players and so many great leaders. And they had some
fantastic coaches as well, so it was the total package. It
really was.

I was so excited to join the team. Ted Watts, the right cornerback, was a rookie. He was an excellent player, don't
get me wrong, but by virtue of him being a rookie, the
opposing teams were going to go after him and pick on
him in certain situations. That's just the nature of football.
As such, they wanted to bring in a veteran to shore up
that 'potential weakness,' and that was what happened.
We had a great secondary though, just outstanding.
Besides Ted, we had Lester Hayes, Mike Davis, Odis
McKinney, and Kenny Hill—we had some guys who
could make big plays.

Another thing that was unique about that team was the fact
that all of our defensive backs were at least 6'0" or taller
and over 200 pounds. We were all fast too—great athletes. That was unheard of in those days. We used that as
extra intimidation. Opposing players knew that not only
were we fast, but we were bigger and could hit hard. So
that all played into the little mind tricks, the head games. If
we could get the other guys thinking about us, rather than

on the routes they were supposed to be running, then that was half the battle.

The Raiders had always had a reputation for being intimidating, and we played right into that. Charlie Sumner, our defensive coordinator, was fantastic. His mind-set was to attack, attack, attack at all times. So we bought into that and tried to be physical and to get opposing players off their games. We wanted to hit hard and make guys have to think twice about running over the middle or doing certain things out on the field. When we were on defense we were never laying back into zone coverage and reading what they were doing. No way. We were attacking at all times. Opposing teams needed to worry about what Charlie was doing, and what coverages he was putting out there, not the other way around. Charlie loved to blitz, and he loved to keep the other guys guessing. He made football fun. Under Charlie, we were going to dictate the flow of the game. That was unique, no question.

The big thing I remember about that team was the fact that after we beat somebody, there weren't any big celebrations or anything like that. We knew that it was just one more win on the way to the ultimate prize, and that was very unique. There was just this overwhelming sense of confidence, like we were supposed to win. When I was playing with the Patriots and we won, guys would celebrate and really cut loose. Whereas with the Raiders it was very different, and that was what made it so special I think.

As for the game itself, it was amazing. We beat the Redskins, 38–9, in Super Bowl XVIII in Tampa. I remember Marcus Allen having a great game—he was the MVP. He ran for nearly 200 yards that day, including an incredible 74-yard touchdown. I had an interception, which was neat, but overall I was just happy to win. I could now officially say that I was a champion. I played for seven more seasons with the Raiders, but that was our only title, so you just never know in this business."

Mike Haynes
CB, Los Angeles Raiders, 1983

Marcus Allen On Distractions
Before Super Bowl XVIII

"Distractions are just a part of the whole Super Bowl experience. In addition to seven guys missing curfew, we almost had an ugly incident one night at a nightclub in Tampa called Confetti's. Both we as well as the Redskins wound up going there one night and ended up having a big staredown in the middle of the club. It could have gotten ugly, but luckily we avoided a confrontation." [1]

"I felt like our early '60s teams were our best teams. Boy, did we ever have some great players in those days—no less than 10 Hall of Famers. There's never been a team that has had 10 Hall of Famers on it, ever, in the history of the NFL. Well, that was our team; we had 10 of the best ever on one roster. It was pretty amazing. The first title team that won it in 1961, that was probably the best one that I played on with the Packers. It was very memorable. We beat the Giants 37–0, so we took care of them pretty good. It could have been 70–0, and I wanted it to be 70–0 to tell you the truth. We were playing at home in Green Bay, and it was colder than hell up there—maybe five degrees, and the wind was just howling. I don't think the Giants were ready for that kind of weather, I really don't. It was just brutal cold. Well, to psych those guys out a little bit, I remember coming out on the field before the game with Jim Taylor in our T-shirts. We warmed up and threw the ball around, just relaxed, having a great time. We could see the Giants players looking down the field at us, wondering if we were either nuts or superhuman, because they were all freezing their asses off. We too were freezing, of course, but we didn't want them to know that. They were all worried about what they were going to wear and about how cold it was, whereas we were worried about executing our game plan.

Needless to say, I think our little pregame exhibition worked. Vince [Lombardi] took out all the starters midway through the third quarter, as to not run up the score. Well, I begged him to put the first team back out there. I wanted to score 70 points that day and really kick their asses. Vince had great respect for the New York Giants though, so he wanted no part of that. He looked at me and yelled, 'Sit down and shut up!' because he knew that would be disrespectful to run it up on them. I remember talking to Frank Gifford about that game years later, and he shared a story with me. He said that in about the third quarter, when we were already up by 30-some points, Giants quarterback Y.A. Tittle wanted to take a breather to warm up. So, he asked the backup, Charlie Conerly, if he wanted to come in for a couple of series. Charlie, who had been freezing his ass off the entire game, just looked up from the bench and said, 'No thanks, Yat. You brought us this far, and you can take us the rest of the way.' Shit, I just about fell on the floor when I heard that from Gif; that was pretty hilarious in my book. Yeah, we really took it to those guys that day. What a great team we had, just fantastic.

We wound up facing those guys again the next year in the championship game as well, this time out in New York at

Paul Hornung carries the ball during Green Bay's 23–12 win over the Cleveland Browns in the 1965 NFL Championship Game. Playing in very muddy conditions, Horning rushed for 105 yards and scored a touchdown. (Vernon Biever/Getty Images)

Yankee Stadium. This one was much closer too; we only won that one 16–7. I remember the field being just horrible that day. In fact, they had just had the circus on the field the day before, and the grass was just brutal. It was a revenge game, but we still came out on top, despite the fact that we played pretty poorly. That's the mark of a great team too in my eyes, when they can come out flat and *still* win the big game. The Giants had some great players in those days, but we were just that much better. That was all there was to it; we were just that good. It didn't matter who we played I think; we were going to beat them those two seasons.

We had a couple of down seasons in '63 and '64 but then got it together in '65 when we beat Cleveland. It was in Lambeau and we won 23–12. They had a helluva team that year and were led by the great Jim Brown. He was the best football player I have ever seen. Period. He brought out our best though because we really wanted to shut him down.

I think the reason we were so good in those days was because of our quarterback, Bart Starr. I think he was the best ever to play the game. He won *five* championships! That's more than Montana, more than Marino, more than Elway, more than Favre—and he never gets that type of respect. He never gets his just-do, and to be honest, that really pisses me off.

Last, but certainly not least, was the championship in '67— the first Super Bowl. We beat the Chiefs in that one out in Los Angles, 35–10, and it was the perfect ending to an otherwise fantastic season. It was a tough game for me personally though because I didn't get to play. You see, I had a pretty bad neck injury and was forced to watch it from the sidelines. When we were up late in the game, Vince asked me if I wanted to go in for one play, just as a decoy, so that I could say I played in the first Super Bowl. I didn't even have to think twice about it. I said, 'Hell no.' I didn't want any part of that; that was bullshit to me. That turned out to be my last game ever, and I wasn't going to go out like that."

Paul Hornung
HB, Green Bay Packers,
1961, 1962, 1965, 1966

"I think the reason we won was because we were able to overcome so much adversity throughout the whole year. We lost Ryan Grant in the first game, and it just seemed like every week it was something else that was thrown at us. Even during the Super Bowl we lost Donald Driver and Charles Woodson, which was really tough because those guys are the leaders of the team. We hung in there as a team though and just believed in ourselves. We even came up with a slogan late in the season, 'Roll Tide,' after the ESPN Alabama commercial. It was a funny thing that we would say to keep each other loose and to just remind us to roll with it and keep it going. Hey, I guess it worked…. Roll Tide!"

Cullen Jenkins
DE, Green Bay Packers, 2010

"The '88–'89 team was a mix of veterans and young guys who were kind of coming into their own at the time. We really came together and started playing as a team midway through that season. The low point came in Arizona where we were up 23–0 in the fourth quarter over the Cardinals and gave up 24 unanswered points to lose the game. That was a galvanizing moment for us. Everybody was so frustrated and upset. There was a lot of anxiety, and we could feel the season potentially slipping away. That game sort of crystallized what we were all about. Ironically, we then lost to the Raiders the following week, but we got it together after that. I remember Ronnie Lott calling a team meeting where we came together and talked about how guys needed to pull their weight more and spend extra time in their studies so they could execute better on game days. When veteran players like that step up and sort of demand a little bit more, guys listen. There became a big focus after that about playing as units, both offensively and defensively. We knew that we had the talent, but we needed to do the extra stuff to get us to that next level. I think guys really started focusing on what we needed to do in order to get to that next level. From there on out we were unbeatable. We went on to beat Minnesota and Chicago in the playoffs and then took care of business by beating the Bengals in the Super Bowl, 20–16, down in Miami. What a feeling, it was absolutely the best. Plus, it was pretty neat to win that game for Bill Walsh too, because we found out afterward that he was retiring. What an amazing football mind he was, just the best.

The '89–'90 season was basically a carryover from the year before. It was as if the season was just extended because we came in and didn't miss a beat. There wasn't a lot of changeover personnel-wise either, so it was basically the same team. Although longtime assistant George Seifert was now the head coach, he fit right in and we really liked him. He didn't make a whole lot of changes, which was nice for us players not to have to learn a new system or anything like that. The execution and level of awareness from guys knowing what needed to be done was at a heightened level. The confidence was there, and the ability to work together was there. Guys were spending extra time

Brent Jones scores on a pass reception against Denver safety Dennis Smith during Super Bowl XXIV. The 49ers defeated the Broncos 55–10. (Andy Hayt/Getty Images)

working on their technique and in the film room. They now knew what it took to become a champion, and it was showing. We went 17–2 that year and just cruised though the playoffs, absolutely burying Minnesota and L.A. before soundly beating Denver, 55–10. I firmly believe that this particular team was the best team in NFL history. I really do. We were awesome. What an honor to be a part of that team. It was truly incredible.

Now, as for the '94–'95 season, that team had a totally different vibe. By now free agency had come into play, and it made it difficult to create that chemistry you used to be able to have when your roster pretty much stayed the same year after year. It became a challenge to integrate the new faces and personalities from other teams into the '49er Way' of doing things. We had some big personalities come on board too, guys like Deion Sanders, Ken Norton, and Rickey Jackson, so I would have to give George Seifert and the entire coaching staff a ton of credit for how they assimilated us all together that year. We started out slow that season, but we got it all figured out shortly after that and never looked back. It was never in doubt from midseason on. Steve Young was in charge as our quarterback and was amazing that season. We flew through the playoffs, beating Chicago and Dallas, and then took care of San Diego in the Super Bowl. We were on a roll; we won by the combined score of 131–69. We just had so much talent on that team it was scary."

Brent Jones
TE, San Francisco 49ers,
1988, 1989, 1994

"We were a very young team in 1973. You see, the Dolphins franchise was founded in '66 and struggled early on, as most new franchises do. Then Don Shula came to town in 1970, and everything changed after that. About 18 rookies made the team that next season, and that would be the nucleus for our two championship teams a few years later. We made it all the way to the Super Bowl in '72, only to lose to an outstanding Dallas Cowboys team, 24–3. They really took it to us that game, and that left a pretty bad taste in our mouths. So, our whole mission that next season was to simply get back to the Super Bowl and then win it. It was never about perfection. That never even became an issue until about the 11th or 12th game of the season. Once we got that far, then it became something we could shoot for.

Not a lot of people know this, but when we went unde-feated in '72 and won the Super Bowl, we were the small-est, lightest team in the league. There were a couple of reasons for that I think. One: the climate in Miami isn't con-ducive for players to carry any excess baggage. It's so hot and humid, you would just about sweat to death in some of those late summer days when the season got started. And two: Don Shula. Don loved to work us hard, and as such, we were always in really good shape. We were built for speed and quickness on both sides of the ball, and that was a big part of our success that year I think. We never lost sight of our goal though, the Super Bowl. The perfect season was just an added bonus as far as we were con-cerned. Beating Washington for the championship, it was an amazing experience—something I will never forget. It was just the perfect ending to the perfect season."

Bob Kuechenberg
OL, Miami Dolphins, 1972, 1973

"Hard work and focus, that was it. We had lost to Dallas the year before, and from the moment we left the field we vowed to get back the next year and avenge that loss. Losing that game was such an empty feeling, and it proved to be a big motivation for us after the fact. Our intensity picked up at training camp, and we were focused on that goal. Sometimes we practiced four times a day—it was brutal. We were just determined though; we were on a mission to get back to the big game and win that damn thing. We had no distractions because nothing else mat-tered. Win after win, we just kept it going week after week.

As the streak grew, the pressure built. We just tried to stay loose and not think about it. Luckily we were a close group; we all genuinely liked each other—which was unique. I remember we would all get together every Thursday after practice for burgers and beers at this hole in the wall to unwind. The owner of the place was a big fan, and he used to make these voodoo dolls of whoever we were playing that Sunday, and we would all stick pins in them. After we won, he would line them up behind the bar and put them on display. It was wild; we used to love going in there and seeing those dolls all lined up. It became sort of a superstitious ritual for us. We just had a lot of characters on that team. Guys were always playing pranks on each other; we just kept things loose. I will never forget the time Manny Fernandez and Larry Csonka put an alligator in Shula's shower stall. My old roomie Kooch [Bob Kuechenberg] and I thought that was pretty hilarious.

So, to see that come to fruition was so meaningful. It's the ultimate satisfaction to achieve the goal you set out to accomplish. To make it even sweeter was the fact that we didn't lose a single game all year. That made it beyond special; that made it historic. I will say this though—yes, we were very good, but we were also very lucky that year. We had some bounces go our way that year, but that's what it takes to win a Super Bowl. You need to catch a few breaks along the way. Everything that needed to happen happened. The football gods were on our side that magical season. We beat Cleveland in the first round of the playoffs and rallied from behind to beat them. Then, even though we were undefeated, we had to go up to Pittsburgh for the AFC Championship Game. The site was predetermined in those days, which was odd. Anyway, we beat them, and then we faced off against Washington in the Super Bowl. And, even though we were 16–0, we were underdogs coming in to the game. How was that possible? We beat them though, 14–7, and just took care of business. I will never forget seeing the words 'BEST EVER' up on a chalkboard after the game in the locker room. Wow, what a feeling.

From there, we just rode that momentum right on through and won it again the following season. We had the whole team back for the most part and just picked up right where we left off. We were so confident. We certainly had a target on our backs though, that was for sure. Teams came gunning for us. Beating Minnesota to go back to back though, that was extremely gratifying. Being from Minnesota, it had extra meaning to me, to beat the team that I had grown up rooting for. To think that those guys lost four Super Bowls really makes you think. You just can't take anything for granted. You know, there are so many great players who have gotten close but have never won it, so I am very humbled when I think about the fact that I have two title rings. It's just a huge honor to be a part of that team and a part of that organization. It was one of the all-time greats, without a doubt."

Jim Langer
C, Miami Dolphins, 1972, 1973

"Looking back, beyond the obvious talent that we had, I think that we just gelled. We had great team camaraderie both on and off the field; guys respected one another. There weren't any locker room issues or big egos or anything like that; we just got along and worked well together. You could tell that there was something special about that team. Even early on, we just clicked. On the field we played well together and stayed healthy too, which was huge. We were extremely confident and felt like nobody was going to stop us. We only had one significant loss that year, to Dallas, but other than that we were pretty much in control the entire way. Coach Gibbs laid out the plan, and we followed it. We believed in ourselves and got the job done. You know, whenever they talk about the greatest teams of all time, we are never mentioned, which I think is totally crazy. That was such a great team. We dominated that year. Our offense was unbelievable, and our defense put up a ton of shutouts. So, I don't get it. In my eyes though, we were one of the best ever."

Chip Lohmiller
K, Washington Redskins, 1991

"The '58 team won because it grew from the 1957 team. That was actually our best team in my eyes. That was when we started learning how to win, which is so important. Good teams find ways to win, and that was what we finally figured out that year. We had a great team in '58 though, and I was very proud to be a member of it."

Gino Marchetti
DE, Baltimore Colts, 1958, 1959

"What made the '86 Giants so unique was the chemistry that we had on that team. This was the pre–free agency era, where teams stuck together for longer periods of time. So you knew from season to season in those days what type of team you were going to have. You knew about players' character, integrity, work ethic, and attitude—you knew who you were going to war with. It was a different mentality than what you see now in the league. Now it's a 'potluck gumbo' approach they take, where they just throw a bunch of stuff against the wall and see what sticks. We had a great team that year though. We crushed the Niners in the opening round of the playoffs, 49–3, and then shut out the Redskins 17–0 at Giants Stadium for the conference championship. In so doing, we became the first team to ever beat a divisional foe three times in the same season. And those guys were good. We were just so determined at that point. From there we headed out to Pasadena for Super Bowl XXI, where we beat the Broncos 39–20. It was unbelievable. We were the champs; what a feeling.

As for the '90 season, that team had a different vibe. We had gone 12–4 the year before and got knocked out of the playoffs by the Rams on a last-second fluke play, so we were pretty hungry the following year. For me, personally, I remember thinking about how I was getting up there in years and about my future. I had averaged 10 sacks or more per season over the past five years as a defensive lineman in a 3-4 defense, which was almost unheard of in those days. I led the team in sacks for three of those years and wanted to be compensated accordingly. So, Lawrence Taylor and I both held out of training camp because we wanted new contracts with salary increases. There we were, 90 percent of our pass rush, down in South Florida fishing and golfing while everybody else was up at camp. That wasn't easy, but we just felt that we had to do what we had to do. I remember rejoining my teammates for the last preseason game though, and once we all reunited, we were on a mission to win that Super Bowl. We had a serious chip on our shoulder.

We were rolling along that season and everything was going great, and then our quarterback Phil Simms broke his foot in mid December in a game against Buffalo. We didn't know what was going to happen, but Jeff Hostetler came in, and we rallied behind him. He took over and did a great job the rest of the way. We beat the Bears, 31–3, to open the playoffs and then headed out to Candlestick Park for the NFC Championship Game to face the two-time defending Super Bowl champion San Francisco 49ers. Sure enough, we hung in there and won the game, 15–13, thanks to Matt Bahr's five field goals. What I remember most about that game was my fourth-quarter sack of Joe Montana, which knocked him out of the game. He wound up breaking his ribs and his hand, it was that bad. I had two sacks and forced two fumbles that game and just felt like I was on a mission, like nothing could stop us. We had beaten a team that had called themselves a 'team of destiny,' which was huge for us. Those 47 guys on my football team just said, 'We're not going to be denied this opportunity. We let this thing pass the year before, but we'll be damned if we let it pass again.' That was our attitude, and we just went in and took care of business.

From there, we carried that momentum right into Super Bowl XXV, where we beat the Bills in a classic. The '91 Super Bowl was amazing. I still get chills thinking about Whitney Houston singing the National Anthem before the game. That was such a tight game—every down was a struggle. I will never forget that last play with eight seconds to go on the clock, when Buffalo had a chance to win it but came up short on Norwood's missed field goal. Wide right! We all went nuts, the party was on. We were champions. You know, we overcame a lot of injuries that season and just persevered. We believed in ourselves, and we did it. We set out to accomplish the goal that we had set early on and did it. It was very gratifying as I look back. My only regret is that we didn't win more. I mean honestly, those teams from '86 to '91, they could have won four straight Super Bowls. No kidding, we were that good. No regrets though. It was such an honor to be a part of those teams and to line up alongside so many great players."

Leonard Marshall
DE, New York Giants, 1986, 1990

"Number one, we had a great defense that year, tops in the league. Well, it's like Lombardi used to say, 'Offense draws a crowd, whereas defense wins you championships.' That was the main reason why we won it, no question. Our defensive coordinator, Walt Michaels, he was a genius. Our offense was pretty darn good too though—nobody could stop us. Joe Namath was amazing that season, and he really stepped up to the plate during the Super Bowl. There was a lot of pressure on him too, a heck of a lot. We had a great receiving corps that year, maybe one of the greatest passing games of all time in Bake Turner, George Sauer, Pete Lammons, and me. I think we only had one busted play with Joe in nine years. We had great chemistry, just fantastic.

I get asked a lot about Joe's now iconic 'prediction' that we were going to win. Joe was a heckuva football player. He was confident for sure, and he liked the ladies, but most of those stories you read about his nightlife—most of that stuff was make believe. Most of those writers just wrote stuff about him so they could get their names in the papers I think. As for that prediction, I think he was just being honest because we all felt very strongly that we could beat them. We used to trade film with the NFL in those days; that was how we scouted each other. Well, we were watching the same Baltimore game over and over again until finally I remember Pete Lammons saying to our coach, 'Weeb [Ewbank], if you keep making us watch this game film, we're going to get overconfident!' We knew we had a good team and liked our chances, provided we didn't make any mistakes. Sure enough, we played them tough the entire game and won, 16–7. We were in control right up until the very end. In fact, Joe didn't attempt one single pass in the fourth quarter. So, it was a great win for us and for the city of New York. Those fans really got behind us that year, and to win it the way we did, it was something else."

Don Maynard
WR, New York Jets, 1968

"We had an awesome team that year. Coach Tomlin had a plan, and we all bought into that plan. We were just really good, from top to bottom. Our offense, our defense, our special teams—we didn't have any weaknesses I don't think. Our offense was dynamic, and we could come from behind; our defense was really tough—everything just went our way that year. We could do everything. We pretty much had every tool imaginable to give our team a chance to win. Beyond that, we had great camaraderie. The guys genuinely liked each other, and we all got along. We were brothers on and off the field; we were a family. That's why we beat the Cardinals that year in the Super Bowl, because we were a family.

Everybody had a role on that team, and everybody was committed to doing their jobs. My role was as the third-down back, but I was willing to do whatever was asked of me. I returned kicks, played on special teams, and just did whatever our coaches needed me to do. Would I have preferred to have been the featured back? Sure, but that wasn't my role. So I just did whatever I could to support the other running backs and help them any way I could. Willie Parker and Rashard Mendenhall and I, we all got along and supported each other. We competed for snaps, but at the same time we encouraged each other as teammates too. It was all about the team. Whatever they needed me to do, I was going to get it done. I prided myself on that. Everybody had that attitude on the team though, which is rare I think, and that was the big reason as to why we were so good. We had a lot of selfless players, team guys. When you have that, then that's when amazing things can happen. That's when teams win championships."

Mewelde Moore
RB, Pittsburgh Steelers, 2008

"The Colts have a tremendous organization, starting with Jim Irsay, the team owner, and Bill Polian, the team president. They made sure to bring in all the right pieces to the puzzle, and in 2007 that started with our head coach, Tony Dungy. Tony was able to put together a great group of assistant coaches who he believed in, and in turn they were able to focus on doing their jobs. We had a very special group of people that season, starting from the top and going all the way down to the bottom. We had some great players to work with, obviously, and I just feel very fortunate to have been a part of that team. We had the best quarterback in the league that year for starters. Peyton Manning is a special ballplayer. His work ethic, his training, his preparation, it's totally unique. A lot of players talk about being great, but Peyton actually does everything that you have to do in order to be great. There's a big difference."

Tom Moore
Offensive Coordinator,
Indianapolis Colts, 2006

"The 1986 Giants, we were the ultimate team. On offense we weren't that flashy; we just had a bunch of workhorses who grinded it out and got it done. Our defense though, it was unbelievable: Lawrence Taylor, Carl Banks, Harry Carson, Gary Reasons, Pepper Johnson, and on and on.

That first Super Bowl we had no doubts about whether or not we were going to win that game. None. We were so confident, we just knew. When I came out of the tunnel in Pasadena I was so pumped up. I could've run through a brick wall. When you get that kind of adrenaline flowing, with that kind of emotion, it was so intense. Everybody just couldn't wait to get out there and just go to work. I will never forget the feeling we all had in the locker room, just that intense feeling of nervous anticipation. We came out flying and beat Denver, 39–20; it was incredible. I remember having some big catches in that game. It was so gratifying to be able to contribute and to be a part of such an amazing team.

In 1991, however, we were hoping for the best. It was totally different than in '87. I remember being so nervous before the game. You have to remember, in 1991 the Gulf War had just started, and everything was different. The security was so tight, and it was a completely different vibe. I remember the emotion on the field when Whitney Houston sang the Star Spangled Banner. Guys were crying—it was so intense. Buffalo was such a good team that year. We weren't nearly as confident going into that championship game as we were the previous one. We had a game plan though, and it worked. We knew that if we were going to have a chance, that we needed to keep that high-powered offense of theirs off the field. So, we just ran the ball all game and hoped for the best. Luckily, it worked out."

Stacy Robinson
WR, New York Giants, 1986, 1990

"Number one, we had really good players. We should have won the championship in '57, but we lost a couple of close ones down the stretch. So, we had a great group of guys who were hungry to get after it in '58. We wound up beating the Giants in the title game that year, and they had a great football team. We even beat them on their home field, which was Yankee Stadium in those days. It was a helluva game, the greatest ever they would call it. We won in the first-ever overtime game too, 23–17. It was something else; I'll never forget it. The next year we lost two of our top running backs to injury in Alan Ameche and L.G. Dupre, and that was tough to recover from. We had the nucleus of guys to pull together though, and that was what we did. Several of our reserve players really stepped it up that season, and that was a big reason why that team won. We beat the Giants again that next year too, this time at old Memorial Stadium in Baltimore. We won 31–16, so it wasn't as close as the year before. They had a good team that year too, but we were just determined. I don't think anybody could have beaten us for that title; we were so confident and so focused. So, to go back to back like that, it was pretty special."

Alex Sandusky
G, Baltimore Colts, 1958, 1959

"We had a single-minded focus to win the world championship. Beyond that, I can sum it up in three words: desire, passion, and destiny. That was it. We had a group of guys who wanted to do something special. We were an out-of-the-box kind of team that year. We didn't do things the way everyone else did; we were totally unique. Where there was a will, there was a way with that group. We were just determined to figure out a way to get it done that year, and we did. We had some big personalities on that team, but we were all able to come together as a unit. You know, a lot of people look at that team and think that we had such great talent. Yes, we did have some good talent, don't get me wrong. I've seen teams come along over the years, offensively in particular, with better talent. But because they weren't 'together,' they didn't win a championship. You need leadership and you need people pulling together, and we had that. It was a special group of guys who were willing to set their egos and everything else aside and come together for the betterment of the team. Once that happens, amazing things can happen."

Mike Singletary
LB, Chicago Bears, 1985

"We never gave up. Throughout the season we had a lot of close games where we were down late, but we never panicked. We knew what we had to do, and it didn't matter if we were down by 28 points or we were down by one point, we never gave up. We knew that all we had to do was to execute our game plan. That was it. We had players and we had the coaches to get it done. We were so confident too; we knew that we were good enough to rally back and win any game that we were playing in. It's a rare feeling, it truly is, and it doesn't happen very often in sports where you get an entire group of guys who all feel that same way and share that. It's special. The 2008 Pittsburgh Steelers had that feeling, and that was why we won the Super Bowl that season. Beyond all of that, we had some great, great players on both sides of the ball. What talent we had on that team, starting of course with our quarterback, Ben Roethlisberger. Just to be able to play alongside a guy like that, what a privilege. Ben's a tough guy. He has a never-give-up attitude, and that rubs off on guys. He's our leader and we feed on that. He's not a guy who says a lot—he leads by example. Players respect that.

He gets beat up and hurt every week, yet he plays through it all and is always there for us. He plays his best at critical moments too, which is so huge. As teammates, when we see that, it just motivates and inspires us to do the same."

Matt Spaeth
TE, Pittsburgh Steelers, 2008

"Winning that first Super Bowl was very special. I remember vividly listening to Coach Lombardi as we prepared for that first title game against Kansas City. In his opening meeting with us, he led off by saying how good he felt the Chiefs were. He told us that not many people were giving them the attention that they deserved. In those days, of course, it was the established NFL and then the upstart AFL. They were the underdogs coming in to this first-ever Super Bowl, and everybody had been predicting that we would win big. Well, Coach wanted us to be extra prepared and to make sure that we didn't take them for granted. He told us that they were larger, stronger, and maybe faster than we were. He reminded us that their coach, Hank Stram, was extremely well prepared, and his team was going to be ready to play. So, we recognized this coming in and put our game plan together accordingly. Coach Lombardi prepared us well, and that was why we were able to win. We beat them 35–10 and played an outstanding game. We had come together as a team and were all extremely proud of what we had accomplished.

Winning that second Super Bowl was extremely gratifying. We came into the '67–68 season as the defending Super Bowl champs and knew that everybody was gunning for us. We knew that it was going to be tough to repeat, but we responded to the challenge. As the quarterback, I felt the pressure, but I just tried to stay focused and execute Coach's game plans. We played well throughout the season and then beat the Rams in the first round of the playoffs. From there, we hosted the Cowboys for the conference championship in what we now know as the 'Ice Bowl.' That was an amazing game, so cold. We came into that game with really positive attitudes though, and I believe that was why we were able to win that game. Heading down to sunny Miami to play in Super Bowl II was quite a reward for winning that game, let me tell you. Once there we faced the Oakland Raiders, who, like the Chiefs, were an outstanding ball club. What I remember most about this game was how exhausted we were coming into it. We had worked so hard just to get there, and we were worried that we had used up all the gas in the tank. After a few days we got it together though, and Coach put together a great game plan for us. We executed it and won the game, 33–14. So to win the first two Super Bowls, it was extremely gratifying. There's nothing else like it."

Bart Starr
QB, Green Bay Packers,
1961, 1962, 1965, 1966, 1967

"Why? Well, for starters we were unbelievably talented. We really were. We had seven future Hall of Famers on our team, so just that there says quite a bit in my eyes."

Bob Stein
LB, Kansas City Chiefs, 1969

"We beat Miami 27–17 in Pasadena that year to win it. What made that team so unique though was that we won it in a strike year. There was a work stoppage that season, which about cut the season in half. While we were off, I remember conducting private practices for about six weeks.

We had over 40 guys show up day in and day out, with no coaches, to take part in them. It was a real commitment by every man on that football team. We were determined to not let the season be a wash. We were also committed to one another in the sense that when the lockout ended, we were going to be ready to go. We knew that some teams would be coming into training camp and getting together for the first time when they reopened the doors and that they would only have a couple of weeks to get in shape and start game planning. Well, we had a huge head start, and in the end it paid off huge for us. So when I think about that season I think about how it started and about how a group of men with one common goal stayed together to fight through a very adverse situation.

As for the game itself, it was an amazing experience. Miami went up early on us 10 3, and we tied it when I was able to find Alvin Garrett for a short touchdown in the second quarter. They then went up 17–10 when Fulton Walker ran back a kickoff 98 yards, which really took the momentum away from us. Moseley kicked another field goal in the third, and then we took the lead for good when John Riggins busted loose on a 43-yard touchdown. It was big. We then iced it late in the game when I hit Charlie Brown on a six-yard touchdown pass. We hung on from there and then started to celebrate.

I have great memories from that game, just fantastic. I have one kind of embarrassing one though that I will never forget. I had just thrown a really bad interception, and as I was walking off the field, I heard my voice over the loudspeakers. I looked up, and there I was, smiling up on the big screen. They decided that this particular moment would be the best time to air a P.S.A. I had shot before the game about the dangers of drunk driving. So, as I am taking the walk of shame over to the sideline, I hear this really annoying, 'Hi, I'm Joe Theismann!' voice, and I just wanted to crawl under a rock.

When you look at the season of 1982, however, you have to first go back and look at the season of 1981. We started out 0–5, and they were going to trade me to Detroit. Luckily that never happened though because Lions quarterback Eric Hipple had a terrific game right around the time they were going to pull the trigger on it. As a result, the deal went south. After we lost to San Francisco in that fifth game, I drove out to Coach Gibbs' house to have a heart-to-heart talk with him. We aired some things out and talked about what needed to change. Things changed in a hurry, and we went 8–3 the rest of the season. It was in those 11 games where we started to develop our personality as a team I think. We made a commitment to become more of a balanced team too, meaning using our great running back John Riggins more and letting him pound it up the middle. We had a great passing game, but we needed more balance to keep opposing defenses honest.

What transpired from all of that was pretty amazing. We carried that momentum into the next season, where, despite the lockout, we picked up right where we left off and ultimately went on to win the Super Bowl. It was an incredible run, it really was. So, to really understand why this team won, you have to go back to the '81 season and see how Coach Gibbs modified the way he approached the game. Remember, he had come out of the West Coast 'throw the ball all over the place' mentality that he had learned under Don Coryell when he was with the San Diego Chargers. We went to a more balanced attack that next year, with big John Riggins shouldering the load, and it worked masterfully.

Every team that has won the Lombardi Trophy has done it with their own unique style. They've been able to do some-

Redskins quarterback Joe Theismann drops back to pass during Super Bowl XVII. Theismann threw two touchdown passes in Washington's 27–17 win over the Miami Dolphins. (Ronald C. Modra/Sports Imagery/Getty Images)

thing different and put their own spin on it to make it theirs. For instance, the Chicago Bears used the 46 defense to win it; the San Francisco 49ers used the West Coast offense to win it; the Baltimore Ravens won it with one of the best defenses in football; the Pittsburgh Steelers won it with their 'Steel Curtain' defense; as for us, we employed a two–tight end offense to win it. So, every team brings something new to the table that other teams had not been used to seeing in order to get there."

Joe Theismann
QB, Washington Redskins, 1982

"Faith and trust. That was it. There was just something very special and unique about that team. Something that not a lot of people know is that our Super Bowl ring is the only one in history that has any kind of declaration or symbolism of faith on it. It says 'FAITH' right on the side, featured very prominently, with 'OUR TIME' on the other side. That really was a big deal to Tony, who went through so much personal adversity in his life around that time. We were such a close team. We genuinely trusted each other, which is such a big factor in a team's overall success. We truly had faith in each other. So, the symbolism for the word 'FAITH' isn't just about religion, it's also about trust—which was really why that team won the Super Bowl that year in my opinion. Faith became such an integral part of that team and that organization throughout those years leading up to the big win. When everybody has faith in each other, and has faith in their coaches, and faith in their organization, great things are possible.

The other big reason why we won it all that year was the fact that we had the best player in the game on our side,

John Riggins On Super Bowl XVII

Riggins rushed for 140 yards and two touchdowns on 36 carries in the NFC Championship Game over Dallas, then set a record in Super Bowl XVII against Miami by rushing for 166 yards on 38 carries.

"You've got to understand the fact that I had never been in a meaningful playoff game in my previous 10 years in the NFL. The Super Bowl is what it's all about. That's the promised land. So, I remember driving into training camp [after retiring and then deciding to make a comeback], and I started thinking about the possibility of winning a Super Bowl and how great that would be. I got goose bumps—the hair was standing up on the back of my neck. I get to camp, and the first guy I see is Joe Bugel [offensive coordinator], and I say, 'Buuuugs! Just give me the ball. That's all I'm gonna say, just give me the ball, and everything's gonna be all right!' This was one of those rare opportunities where you had a chance to step forward and basically shape your destiny, and I will always feel like that was my moment.

For John Riggins the athlete, maybe for John Riggins the man, that was my favorite story of all time. Beating Dallas to go to the Super Bowl, that was a very defining moment for us in knowing that we were going to the Super Bowl. Winning the Super Bowl, meanwhile, that was more of a numbing, stunning moment.

I was the last guy to leave the stadium that night after we won. The stands were completely empty by the time I left, just workers cleaning up all the garbage from the stands. I remember walking out onto the field and looking up at the scoreboard afterward and reading 'Redskins 27, Dolphins 17.' In that moment I said to myself, 'I'm a world champion.' That was it. That was what it was all about." [2]

Peyton Manning. Peyton is the ultimate student of the game. He works so hard and studies so hard, it's no wonder he's the best quarterback in football. To have played with him was such an honor and privilege. He was so good at helping his teammates to elevate themselves to become the best that they could be. He was the best player I ever played with, without a doubt. It's hard not to be successful when you are around a guy like that. Peyton is just a really good guy. We shared a lot of the same interests and values, and I think that was why we got along so well. I was proud to be his teammate, but I'm even more proud to be his friend."

Ben Utecht

TE, Indianapolis Colts, 2006

"That was a great team. We had a lot of younger veterans on that team. There was a bunch of us who were in our fifth and sixth years in the league at that time. That's the perfect age; you've been around the block a few times, and you know what to expect. You're older, but you're not too old. You're not completely worn out yet. Free agency wasn't like it is today back then either, so we had most of the same guys back on the roster year after year. What that did was to build chemistry. We liked each other. Our confidence level was strong, and we just knew that we were a good football team. We only lost one game all season. Plus, we had that Raider mystique. We enjoyed being physical and intimidating. We enjoyed the fact that other teams feared us in many regards. That bonded us and gave us an identity. Beyond that, we stayed pretty healthy. That's always the wildcard in this business, staying healthy. We could have won a whole bunch of Super Bowls I think, but the next year we had tons of injuries. We could just never recover from it, and it ultimately cost us. So, it was a lot of things that led to us winning it, but for the most part it was just our year. Everything came together and fell into place for us. To win a Super Bowl, that's the kind of stuff that has to happen. They're rare for a reason."

Phil Villapiano
LB, Oakland Raiders, 1976

"That late '70s, that was our time. The Steelers were a dynasty in those days. Why did those teams win? It was a combination of a little bit of luck and a whole lot of hard work. We had some talented players on those teams, that's for sure. Great coaches, too. And we had the Steel Curtain defense, which allowed us to be able to set the tone defensively. I just think we were better on those given days, those key playoff games and championship games. We had some great game plans and were able to execute them when it mattered most. That was it. We were prepared both mentally and physically and had confidence in ourselves. Look, there were many great players on many great teams during that era, and I want to acknowledge them too, but that was just *our* time."

Mike Wagner
S, Pittsburgh Steelers,
1974, 1975, 1978, 1979

"The 1984 team was a special team with just an incredible group of guys. I had just come to San Francisco from Dallas that season, where I had gotten cut the year before as a rookie. I was excited about playing for the Niners though and was thrilled to be playing for a team that actually wanted me. I wound up playing linebacker behind Hacksaw Reynolds, who was near the end of his career. He would play on the run-only downs, and then I would come in for the passing downs. I normally didn't play that much, but in Super Bowl XIX we played Miami, who passed a lot—so I got to see a lot of action. It was awesome. We won the game 38–16, and I remember just not wanting the game to end. I was having so much fun out there, completely enjoying the moment. I just didn't want it to stop. What an amazing feeling. The game was at Stanford too, right in our own backyard, which made it even that much more special for our fans. We had a great team that year. We just came out, competed, and won. It was a great group of guys that genuinely liked each other and got along great. There were no racial problems, no big egos, nothing. Of all the teams I would play on over my career, this was my favorite. Just the satisfaction of knowing the year before that the Dallas Cowboys basically said that I lacked the skills necessary to play in this league, and here I was holding the Lombardi Trophy. That was a pretty gratifying moment in my life.

The 1988 season, where we beat Cincinnati in the Super Bowl down in Miami, will always be remembered for 'The Drive.' This iconic, intense, last-minute 12-play, 92-yard drive down the length of the field to win the game. Well, one of the great stories about it came during a timeout midway through the series. Right in the middle of this incredible, stress-filled drive, where everybody was on edge, Joe [Montana] comes back to the huddle following the break and sees how uptight everybody was. So, to loosen them up, he says, 'Hey guys, look over there in the front row, that's [actor] John Candy!' It was unbelievable. Here we are, in the biggest moment of the season, with the game on the line, and the quarterback is stargazing. It was hilarious. What it did though, is it broke the ice and got everybody to relax, just for a moment. Joe wanted everybody to chill out and refocus; he knew that we weren't going to be able to win with everybody so nervous. Well, sure enough, we went on and scored the game-winner in dramatic fashion when Joe hit John Taylor on a 10-yard touchdown with just over 30 seconds left to give us the 20–16 victory. It was epic. It was just the perfect way to end an amazing season.

We carried the momentum from the '88 season right into the '89 season too, as we went back-to-back and beat Denver, 55–10. It was just a blowout. I remember talking to some of the guys during halftime about what we were going to do after the game out in New Orleans. It was crazy. I wound up picking off [John] Elway late in the game for an interception, which was one of the highlights for me personally. Really though, it was just a complete team win. Everybody pitched in that season, and it solidified us as a true dynasty. To make it two in a row in those days was no easy task, and we had not only done it, but done it in style. I have so many great memories from those teams; we just had so many talented players. What a well-oiled machine we had going in those days. Amazing.

We actually should have won a third the next year, but we were upset by the Giants in the NFC Championship Game. That was such a bitter pill to swallow; I will never forget it. I remember we had the lead and the ball in our possession with a just few minutes to go in the game. We were just running the clock out with Joe handing the ball off to [running back] Roger Craig. Lawrence Taylor then came off the corner, like only he could do, and knocked the ball out of

Roger's hands. They recovered the fumble and then went on to beat us with a game-winning field goal with no time left on the clock. Just like that, there went the three-peat. What a horrible moment, absolutely brutal."

Mike Walter

LB, San Francisco 49ers,
1984, 1988, 1989

"We overcame a Baltimore team at Municipal Stadium in Cleveland that was favored by 17 points and beat them 27–0. They had Johnny Unitas and Gino Marchetti and Raymond Berry, just a whole bunch of Hall of Famers, and we took it to 'em. It was such a special day, I'll never forget it. There were some things that had to happen that day in order for us to win, and they did happen. I went back and watched the game film afterward and was just blown away. For starters, our starting linebacker and captain, Galen Fiss, seemingly played a perfect game—if there is such a thing. He made some great, great plays and was solid on every down. Our star running back, Jim Brown, played marvelously. He was the great equalizer, just an amazing ballplayer. Gary Collins was the MVP in the game because of all the phenomenal plays he made that day, including three touchdowns. He was everywhere, all over the field. Jim Kanicki, an unknown defensive tackle who was filling in for former Outland Trophy winner Bob Gain, had to go up against Jim Parker, the future Hall of Fame guard, and he won the battle. It was incredible.

Everybody, from top to bottom, came through and did what he had to do that day. Frank Ryan was our quarterback, and the guy was brilliant. He had a PhD in geometric function theory and an IQ of about 200. He was a completely different guy, but a heck of a football player. All in all we were huge underdogs that day, but we somehow prevailed. We were challenged in a lot of areas, but we answered the bell. Every once in a while in athletics things go right, they go your way. On this day, for whatever the reason, things went our way. It had nothing to do with the referees or anything like that either; there was no luck involved. It was just a case of every man doing his job to the best of his abilities and refusing to let his teammates down. From there we caught a few breaks, and the rest is history. It was tied 0–0 at halftime, and everybody thought that Baltimore was going to come and destroy us in the second half, but instead it was us that did the destroying—scoring 27 unanswered points to put it away. It was remarkable."

Paul Wiggin
DE, Cleveland Browns, 1964

We were a close-knit team. It started in camp—everybody worked so hard; nobody complained. That attitude just sort of blossomed throughout the season. Everybody got along so well that year too. I was just a second-year player at the time, but the veteran guys all made me feel like I belonged. I even had a locker next to Lawrence Taylor and Carl Banks, which was pretty intimidating to say the least. All the guys on the offensive line, we were all good buddies. Us linemen, we were the core of the offense. It was our job to protect the quarterback; it was our job to open holes for the running back. We were on a mission, and we just clicked that year. We worked hard and never gave up either. In fact, we won seven games that year by a field goal or less. That to me proved without a doubt that we never gave up on ourselves. We just kept battling and never quit. Guys stepped up when they had to. Our star quarterback Phil Simms went down that year, and Jeff Hostetler was huge for us. He performed unbelievably, he really did. We had great coaches too. Coach Parcells pushed us and challenged us, and we responded. Everything worked out in the end, and we just believed in ourselves. It was just a magical season, it truly was."

Brian Williams
OL, New York Giants, 1990

Drew Brees On Winning Super Bowl XLIV for New Orleans

"Four years ago, who ever thought this would be happening? I mean, 85 percent of the city was underwater. People were evacuating to places all over the country. Most people left not knowing if New Orleans would ever come back, or if the organization would ever come back. Not only did the organization come back, the city came back. And so many players, our core group of players that came in that year as free agents, we just all looked at one other and said, 'We are going to rebuild together. We are going to lean on each other.' That's what we've done the last four years, and this is the culmination of all that belief.

Really, over the last four years since I've been in New Orleans, to be given the opportunity there when not a lot of people wanted to give me that opportunity, and to really start from scratch building a team, building a mind-set and setting those goals we knew we could achieve through hard work and trusting one another. What can I say? We played for so much more than just ourselves; we played for our city. We played for the entire Gulf Coast region. We played for the entire 'Who-Dat' nation that has been behind us every step of the way. We've been blessed with so much. It's unbelievable."

CHAPTER
3

Defining
Moments

Beyond why *that* team won the championship, in this chapter I wanted to dive deeper to learn about specific events that may have acted like catalysts in the team's success. I wanted to better understand how big wins, big losses, big injuries, and big moments were able to play roles in the team's success. From off-season training camp fights, to players overcoming injuries and playing through adversity, to backup players stepping up in big games—every team had a defining moment somewhere along the way that sparked the team and got their momentum moving forward. Once that momentum got going, like a freight train, it simply couldn't be stopped. Teams that have that kind of energy become "teams of destiny."

WAS THERE A DEFINING MOMENT FROM THAT SEASON, AN EVENT THAT SWUNG THE MOMENTUM AND PLAYED A FACTOR IN THE TEAM'S SUCCESS?

"The defining moment for us in 1992, my first Super Bowl, was when played at Philadelphia in Week 5 on *Monday Night Football*. They owned the division in those days. Up

Dallas Cowboys quarterback Troy Aikman throws a pass during the second quarter of Super Bowl XXX. Aikman led the Cowboys to three Super Bowl championships. (AP Images)

until that point those guys would always beat our brains in, especially defensively. We could just never move the ball against them. Well, they beat us, but we were finally able to get a few first downs. It was one of the only times I could ever remember really feeling good about a loss. So, that was a game for us that gave us a great deal of confidence moving forward.

The big moment for me in that first Super Bowl against Buffalo [1993] came early in the fourth quarter. I had just thrown a touchdown pass to Alvin Harper and knew that the lead was too much for them to come back from at that point and that we were going to win it. I remember jogging to the sideline after that and seeing all the guys hugging and jumping around, celebrating, and just knowing that we were going to be world champions. That's what I think about. It's not one play; it's not a touchdown; a particular call; a big speech; it was seeing those other 52 guys along with the equipment managers, the trainers, and the coaches, everybody just celebrating what it was we were there to do. Having gone 1–15 just three years prior, it was a pretty amazing feeling. You know, I have always said that I really feel bad for anyone who has played this game for any length of time who has not experienced what it is like to win a Super Bowl. It's the ultimate." [1]

Troy Aikman
QB, Dallas Cowboys,
1992, 1993, 1995

The Greatest Feeling in the World

"For all you players and coaches, understand this: as much as you relish being the best, as good as it feels, the best thing that you've got and will have for the rest of your life is the love that you have from one another right now—because that's what got you here. It's about being a total team. That feeling, it's something that you will never ever lose. It's the greatest feeling in the world. Congratulations!" [2]

Jimmy Johnson
Head Coach, Dallas Cowboys,
1992, 1993

"The defining moment for us that season was when we beat Chicago. They had the No. 1 defense in the league that year, and we were just able to put it all together that day. It was a huge win and gave us a lot of confidence I think. It really propelled us and gave us a lot of momentum, which we were able to ride all the way through the playoffs."

Jerome Bettis
RB, Pittsburgh Steelers, 2005

"I think the defining moment in the game for us was when we opened the second half with an onside kick. We had talked about the kick, 'Ambush,' as it was known, for the two weeks leading up to the big game. We worked on it every day in practice, and for Sean [Payton, head coach] it wasn't if we were going to run it, but when we were going to run it. We were only down by four at that point, and Sean figured that we would catch them with the element of surprise. I mean the last thing that anybody thought was that we would open the half with a trick play, but what a moment-changer it was. That gave us so much confidence, and from there we went right down and scored to take the lead, 13–10. Having been down 10–0 at one point early on, we finally felt like we could win this game after that. Sean trusted us to run that play, and as players we responded to that. If he believes in us enough to run that play in this situation, then we knew we had to respond. The message it sends to the team is that you know what, we're going to pull out all the stops. We're not holding anything back; we're going to make a run at this thing." [3]

Drew Brees

QB, New Orleans Saints, 2009

"[The final drive of the 2008 Super Bowl] was an amazing drive in that we'd make a first down and then we'd stall for a few plays. And then we'd make another one, and obviously I'm trying to conserve my timeouts. But there's a couple of situations where I can't—with a sack, the clock would have run forever, and you've got to use them—now we have no timeouts. But before I say anything about that, the escape by Eli and the throw caught by David Tyree—that ball was challenged. That wasn't like he just jumped up in the air and caught the ball. That was challenged; you had two people, ripping for the ball, and he brings it down. That might be one of the great plays of all time in the Super Bowl.... And then when you're out of timeouts, and Steve Smith's tight in was a big one, getting that first down was a big one there. And then they came with the blitz, which we knew would come eventually, and he went on the fade to Plaxico. I couldn't tell if he was in or out. I didn't know where the ball was until the reaction of the crowd. It was amazing to me, and I looked and I said, 'Holy cow, there's still 35 seconds left here.'" [4]

Tom Coughlin
Head Coach, New York Giants, 2007

"Beating Minnesota at home that year early in the season. We were 3–3 and really struggling at that point, but when we beat those guys, a big divisional rival, that really gave us a shot of adrenaline. We won 28–24 up at Lambeau, and Aaron [Rodgers] had a big game, throwing for nearly 300 yards and a couple of touchdowns. I remember Randy Moss scoring late, which was interesting, but we held them down the stretch and took care of business. We carried that momentum with us and went on a four-game winning streak, which really got us back on track."

Mason Crosby
K, Green Bay Packers, 2010

"The defining moment for us that season [1985 Bears] was without a doubt when we got beat by Miami on *Monday Night Football*. That made us realize that we weren't perfect, that we were going to have to work even harder. It humbled us I think, which was what we needed at that point in the season. It refocused us. We struggled to win our next two games, but from there on out we were unstoppable. We went on a roll, and it didn't end until we were world champions."

Mike Ditka
TE, Dallas Cowboys, 1971;
Head Coach, Chicago Bears, 1985

"I think that there were two defining moments in 2006. The first was the loss to Jacksonville in December where we got beat 44–17. People were writing us off after that, figuring that there was no way we could rebound from that loss and win the Super Bowl. We stuck together though, we didn't panic, and we worked a little bit harder.

Indianapolis Colts coach Tony Dungy hoists the Lombardi Trophy for fans during a Super Bowl rally at the RCA Dome in Indianapolis following the Colts' 29–17 win over the Chicago Bears in Super Bowl XLI. (AP Images)

We decided that one loss was not going to define us. Then, the second moment was in the AFC Championship Game when we were down 21–3 against New England and rallied back to win, 38–34. We had been there so many times against those guys and been so close, only to come up short. So, we were really determined and had so much resolve not to fall short again, and we dug deep. We came together again and just got it done—it was an amazing accomplishment. It just lets you know that you can't just take a snapshot at any one point during a season and say it's going to be a success or a failure. You have to fight all the way through. This team certainly realized that, and that was why they ended the year as Super Bowl champions."

Tony Dungy

DB, Pittsburgh Steelers, 1978;
Head Coach, Indianapolis Colts, 2006

"For me it was when we went down to Dallas in Week 11 and beat the Cowboys as convincingly as we did. That was the turning point in my eyes. They were a good team, and this was a real test for us. A lot of people in the media were saying, 'We'll find out what the Bears are made of on the road against America's Team.' Well, we just demolished them, 44–0, it wasn't even close. Our chests really began to get puffed up out there at the end; we were feeling pretty confident after that. We knew that we had a chance to be something special if we could keep it going that season. I remember shutting out Atlanta the next week, only to get beat by Miami the following Monday night. That would turn out to be our only loss that season, and it humbled us a little bit I think. Looking back, it was probably a good thing for us, to knock us back down to earth a little bit. We got back on track the next week and just rode that momentum all the way to the Super Bowl."

Leslie Frazier
CB, Chicago Bears, 1985;
Assistant Coach, Indianapolis Colts, 2006

"I think it was the big win over the Giants in Week 16. We had lost the previous two games and knew that our fate was in our own hands at that point. It was up to us to determine how far we would go with two weeks left in the regular season. We were pretty much in a lose-and you're-out playoff situation, but we were able to come together and beat those guys by a pretty good margin, 45–17. That gave us a lot of confidence because they were a good team. We never looked back from there. We beat the Bears that next weekend at home and then had to go on the road for all three playoff games: Philly, Atlanta, and Chicago. From there we hung on to beat the Steelers and win the championship. So, I think that game over the Giants, where if we lost we were done, really propelled us and got our momentum going."

Cullen Jenkins
DE, Green Bay Packers, 2010

"We started out kind of lackluster that season. We knew that we had all the ingredients to win but lacked the sense of urgency early on, for whatever the reason. I think the defining moment for us came after our third loss of the season, against the Bears. Afterward we got together as a team and made a commitment to one another that every day we would challenge each other to be the best we could be. It was like a light bulb went off because we got turned around and came together after that. In fact, we didn't lose another game for the rest of the season, winning 10 straight games en route to beating Miami in the Super Bowl."

Lee Roy Jordan
LB, Dallas Cowboys, 1971

"The first Super Bowl in 1967 was probably the most memorable of all five championships, because it was such a historic game to be a part of. There was a lot of pressure on Coach Lombardi at that time because we knew he was getting calls from the old guard of the NFL and that there was some animosity between the AFL and the NFL regarding the merger at that time. Because there was so much pressure on him, he wound up putting a lot of extra pressure on us, and we could feel it.

Before we could play the Chiefs in Super Bowl I, however, we had to first get past the Cowboys. It was just unbelievable, it really was. It was bitter, bitter cold, but that didn't bother me too much due to the fact that I had grown up in Idaho and was used to playing in that type of weather. What a thrilling game though—it all came down to that final drive. Prior to that, we hadn't been able to do a damn thing either. In fact, we had 10 possessions, ran 31 plays, and made a whopping minus nine yards. No kidding. I even had our play-by-play announcer look it up for me just to be sure because I couldn't believe it either. It all came down to that final 65-yard drive though, and thankfully we were just able to get it into the end zone.

We of course won the game, 21–17, and I remember asking Bart [Starr] what made him think we could go 65 yards when we had been getting shut down for so long up until that point of the game. He said, 'I looked in your eyes. I looked in Forrest's [Gregg] eyes.' And he went on and on. He could see it in our eyes, that we were hungry and that we had come this far. He did not want to let us down, and he certainly didn't want to let Coach Lombardi down. We were going to win the first Super Bowl no matter what it took. He just knew that we had to reach down and dig deep, so we all just sort of jumped on his back that afternoon. We could see his resolve, his pride, and we all knew that he was going to get the job done. Somehow, some way, he was determined, and he willed us down the field. When I threw that block for him on the last play, I just knew he was going to get in. I just knew it. When we dug deep and reached down, we found Lombardi, all of his principles, all of his teachings, and all of the things that he stood for. Looking back, that's what took us down the field that day. I really believe that. That drive personified Coach Lombardi and everything he stood for. He was definitely our motivation.

I would say that the second Super Bowl was very significant too, in that it would ultimately turn out to be Coach Lombardi's last game ever with the Packers. Getting through the playoffs that year was no picnic. We first beat the Rams, who had the 'Fearsome Foursome' and just one helluva football team. Then we played Dallas, who also had a helluva football team with their 'Doomsday Defense.' From there we faced off against the AFL champs from Oakland in the Super Bowl. We felt like they were a good football team but not as good as the Rams or Cowboys. The AFL had some great ballplayers in those days, but we just felt like we could handle them. Anyway, we beat them, 33–14, down in Miami.

We played great, and everything just seemed to go our way. It was our fifth championship in eight years, so to say we had a dynasty in those days is an understatement. Like I said, it would prove to be Lombardi's last ever game with the franchise, and for that reason it was historic. We didn't find that out officially until a few days later, but when we did it was certainly big news. For health reasons, he wanted to step down and serve as the team's general manager. So, our

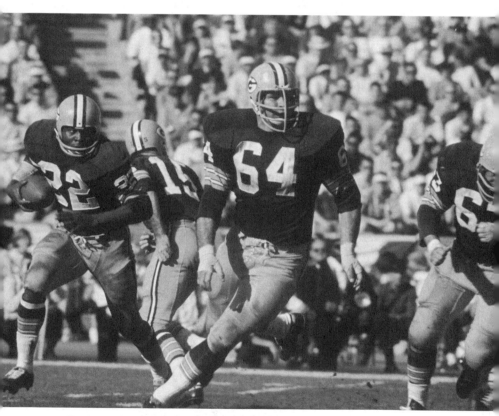

Packers guard Jerry Kramer leads the blocking for running back Elijah Pitts during the Packers' 35–10 win over the Kansas City Chiefs in Super Bowl I. The Hall of Famer was a member of five Packers teams that won the NFL championship. (James Flores/Getty Images)

defensive coordinator Phil Bengtson took over that next year. We went 6–7–1 that next year, and things went south from there. I decided to retire shortly thereafter. It was a helluva ride though, one of the best ever. Looking back, all I have is great memories and a whole bunch of lifelong friendships. What more could you ask for?"

Jerry Kramer
G, Green Bay Packers,
1961, 1962, 1965, 1966, 1967

"I would say there were two during the 1972–73 season. The first was rallying to beat the Vikings in the third game of the year up in Minnesota. They were so tough in those days, especially their defense led by the dreaded 'Purple People Eaters.' There was five minutes left in the game, and we were down by eight. There was no two-point conversion in those days, so we needed two scores. We drove down, and Garo Yepremian hit the longest field goal of his career, a 51-yarder, to cut the lead to five. Our defense held, and Jim Mandich wound up scoring the game-winner in the game's final moments—it was unbelievable. That was probably the only game of the season that we were not in control. We never lost our cool though and just hung in there until the end.

The second one was beating the Steelers in the AFC Championship Game. You see, there was no home field advantage in those days, and despite the fact that we were undefeated at 15–0 and had the best record in football, we had to play the game on the road in Pittsburgh, in December. How unheard of is that? We beat them though, 21–17, to advance to the Super Bowl. Once we got past those guys up there, and that 'Steel Curtain,' we knew that we could beat anybody.

As for the next season, when we repeated, I'm not sure if there was a defining moment that year or not. We were just really damn good! Even though we didn't go unde-feated again, we were a much better team in my eyes. We were still a young team, but we had matured and had so much more confidence. I remember at each playoff game that year we won all three coin tosses to start the game. We elected to take the ball, and on each opening drive we went down and very methodically scored. Each drive took between five and eight minutes and included 15–18 plays, and each one ended with seven points. It was amazing. We didn't know it at the time, but the game was over at that point. We just knew that we weren't going to relin-quish the lead from then on; we were just so confident in our abilities as a team."

Bob Kuechenberg
OL, Miami Dolphins, 1972, 1973

"When we lost our starting quarterback, Bob Griese, for most of that 1972 season, we really had to dig deep. Earl Morrall came in though, and we rallied behind him. I remember him trotting out to the huddle for that first play, and he just looked at us and said, 'Okay men, let's go to work.' He was confident and determined to keep it going. What he did, filling in for the Grease Man the way he did, it was incredible. Earl was in his late 30s at that point and had slowed down a bit. He wasn't as nimble as Bob was, but he was just as smart—if not smarter. Having Earl out there was like having another offensive coordinator. He had played for Shula in Baltimore and knew that system better than anybody. We put everything we had behind him though, and that became our new focus. We knew that we had a great running game and a great defense. So, we figured as long as he didn't lose any games for us, that we would be in every one of them. We all just kicked it up a notch. Sure enough, he came through and played just fantastic. In fact, he got 11 of the 17 wins we had that year. Amazing. That was a very unselfish team in every sense of the word. We were just so focused on winning that year that we literally ate, slept, and lived football. That was it."

Jim Langer
C, Miami Dolphins, 1972, 1973

"I would say it was winning the Western Division crown in '58 when we beat San Francisco in Baltimore City. What made that game so important for us was the fact that we were able to rally and come from behind to win. They were ahead 27–7 at halftime, and we came back to beat them 35–27. It was probably the most excited I had ever been after a game—it was something else. We went on to win the championship the next month in New York, and I think the reason why we were able to do that was because of the confidence and momentum that we had built in the win over the Niners. It was just a great, great comeback. John Unitas played outstanding, Lenny Moore had some fantastic runs in that second half, and everybody played great. What a great feeling—I will never forget it."

Gino Marchetti
DE, Baltimore Colts, 1958, 1959

"One of the biggest disappointments that season was when we lost up in Buffalo in Week 3. I remember Coach Ewbank telling the pilot to fly over Niagara Falls on the way up there so we could see it. Maybe he thought it was going to be an easy win for us, so he took us sightseeing, but boy was he wrong. Joe [Namath] threw nine touchdowns that afternoon: four to us and five to them. We got beat 37–35, and it really threw us for a loop. That wound up being the only game that the Bills would win all year. We took them for granted and got a little cocky. It cost us. We got together after that and had a team meeting to sort things out. I remember our offensive coordinator telling Joe to quit throwing the ball and just let the defense handle things. Sure enough, Joe never threw a single touchdown pass over the next six games. We were just very careful from there on out and played the game like you're supposed to, with balance."

Don Maynard
WR, New York Jets, 1968

"I would say there were two big defining moments for us that season. The first came at Heinz Field during the AFC Championship Game against Baltimore when Troy Polamalu had the big interception toward the end of the game and took it all the way to the house to ice it. Now, the second one is going to sound self-serving because it involves me, but it was a total team effort…trust me. It came in Week 4, also against the Ravens, when all three of our starting running backs got hurt, and I wound up having to shoulder the entire load. I'm normally a third-down back, but I filled in that game and was able to help us win down the stretch. I remember converting on a key third down and helping to get us into field-goal position where we were able to win it in overtime. It was a huge win for us. I think that momentum just catapulted us through the middle of our season. It ultimately got us home field advantage for the playoffs too, which was big because our fans at home are just incredible."

Mewelde Moore
RB, Pittsburgh Steelers, 2008

"The defining moment to me was in the AFC Championship Game against the Patriots. We were so far behind in that game, I think nearly everybody had written us off. To come back and win it though, the way that we did, it was incredible. One of the great wins of my entire career, without a doubt. You know, we always say, 'It's who goes the hardest, the longest…,' and in that game it was the Colts. We waited until the clock read 59:32 before we scored the final touchdown to seal the victory. What a game. It was the culmination of so much hard work and so many long hours. I will just never forget it. What it did though is catapult us right into the Super Bowl, where we were able to ride that momentum and defeat the Chicago Bears."

Tom Moore
Offensive Coordinator,
Indianapolis Colts, 2006

"That was a team of guys who all came together at the right time. I remember starting out 1–3 that year, and it was pretty bleak. Then, one day during a team meeting after practice, Mickey Marvin went up to the chalkboard and wrote 2–3, followed by 11–5. He put it up there for all of us to look at and basically said that if we got our act together, we could go all the way. It seemed pretty far-fetched at the time, but sure enough, we dug in and finished the year 12–5 as Super Bowl champions. It was definitely a defining moment for us that year. We wound up beating the Eagles 27–10 in New Orleans. I remember Jim Plunkett played great, and Rod Martin had three interceptions. What a way to end the season, just amazing. We had a lot of very talented players, but we didn't have any big superstars on the team. Everybody just worked hard, and we did what we had to do."

Bob Nelson
DT, Oakland Raiders,
1980; Los Angeles Raiders, 1983

On the 1991 Giants: "I think the defining moment for us this year was when our starting quarterback, Phil Simms, broke his foot during a game against Buffalo toward the end of the season. His backup, Jeff Hostetler, took over, and the press was all over him—it was crazy. They basically wrote us off, figuring with Simms out we would just fall apart. It was like nobody believed in Jeff but us. We knew that he could get the job done though; we were behind him 100 percent. He responded big time and did a really great job for us. We won our final two games of the year and then swept through the playoffs, beating the Bills in the Super Bowl, 20–19. What an ending to that game, right down to the final play. Sitting there and watching that kick sail wide with time running off the clock, knowing we had won the Super Bowl—it was a moment I will never forget. So, without Jeff stepping up the way he did, we never would have won it that year. It was such an incredible run."

On the 1987 Giants: "I remembering being up in Minnesota in Week 11 playing the Vikings, and it was fourth-and-17 late in the game. Phil Simms hit Bobby Johnson on a sideline route to pick up the first down, and it sealed it for us. Raul Allegre came in to kick the 33-yard game-winner, and we won 22–20. I just knew from that moment on that we weren't going to be stopped from there on out. Sure enough, we didn't lose another game all season."

Stacy Robinson
WR, New York Giants, 1986, 1990

"For me there were two defining moments. The first was actually the last game of the '84 season when we lost the NFC Championship Game to San Francisco 23–0. We had a good team, but not great. We had a great running back, a good offensive line, and an outstanding defense. We didn't have a consistent quarterback at that time though and knew coming into that next year that we were going to need a new leader under center if we were going to have a chance at winning it. We had gained so much confidence by getting that far though, and we knew that we were close. We just felt like we needed that one missing piece to the puzzle. At the end of that game we had hunger. We were so passionate and driven after that game, it was incredible. So, those were the two big things, confidence and hunger, and they were coming together at just the right time for us. We were the youngest team in the league at that time too, so we knew that if we could just add that piece that we were going to get there. Sure enough, the next year we were able to get Jim McMahon in there and got it done.

The second one came following our only loss of the year, to Miami on Monday night. A lot of people don't know this, but we actually taped the 'Super Bowl Shuffle' the next morning. Guys were really reluctant to go and do it, but we had committed to it and we did it. Now, the 'Shuffle' wasn't a distraction in my eyes, but it certainly could've been. I think if we'd won that game, it could have been a disaster because we probably would've felt like there was no way in the world that anybody could stop us. We came back to Earth pretty quickly after that loss though. Looking back, the timing was outstanding because we were feeling horrible about the game, and that video sort of brought us out of that fog. Instead of whining about the game and pointing fingers, it made us take a step back and collect ourselves. Needless to say, we refocused after that and didn't lose another game all year."

Mike Singletary
LB, Chicago Bears, 1985

"Two big ones come to mind. The first came early in the season when we got beat pretty badly by New England. Afterward Gene Upshaw and Willie Brown addressed the team and said, 'Okay, that's it, we're not losing any more this year. We're gonna work hard, and we're gonna practice hard every day, and we're going to the glory land.' All 50-some guys went out and busted their butts day in and day out the rest of the way, and guess what? We didn't lose another game that entire season. The second one came in the playoffs when we got revenge on the Patriots and advanced on to play Pittsburgh in the AFC Championship Game. The Steelers were so tough in those days. You didn't bring one lunch with you when you played Pittsburgh; you needed to bring two, because those guys battled you hard right up to the end. We didn't like those guys, and they didn't like us. So, when we got past them that was a real turning point. It gave us a lot of confidence, and we used that to propel past Minnesota in the Super Bowl. I remember kissing that trophy afterward in the locker room—it was a moment I will never forget. We wanted to win it for John [Madden]. That was the most important thing in our eyes, to win it for Coach. We saw how happy he was after the game and all felt really good about that, without a doubt."

Otis Sistrunk
DE, Oakland Raiders, 1976

Otis Sistrunk sacks Vikings quarterback Fran Tarkenton during Oakland's 32–14 win over Minnesota in Super Bowl XI. (Vernon Biever/Getty Images)

"Beating the Baltimore Ravens for the third time that season, in the AFC Championship Game, that was the big moment for us in my eyes. They're huge rivals for us, and for us to beat them three times in one season was unbelievable. They had a great team that season, with so much talent, so once we did that we just knew that we had what it took to go all the way. We knew that if we could get past that scary defense that we could get past anybody."

Matt Spaeth
TE, Pittsburgh Steelers, 2008

"There were two big things I remember from that season that were pretty defining for our team. The first was when [quarterback] Len Dawson got hurt early in the season. It was about four games in, and he hurt his knee. Then our backup quarterback, Jacky Lee, broke his leg in his first game. So, we ended up playing four or five really tough games with our third-string quarterback, Mike Livingston, and we wound up winning them all. That was just huge. Everybody liked Livvy, and we rallied behind him. It was incredible.

Then, the other big thing that year was beating Oakland in the playoffs. We hated those guys and visa versa. As the old saying goes, we could have played those games without a football. We really got up for those guys; they were always really physical games. They had beaten us twice during the regular season, so when we beat them in the playoffs on their home field, we knew that we were a team of destiny. I will never forget toward the end of the game when Raiders defensive end Ben Davidson speared [Chiefs quarterback] Lenny Dawson and then kind of rolled up on

him when he was down. That started a huge brawl
between the two teams and was pretty intense."

Bob Stein

LB, Kansas City Chiefs, 1969

"I would say that there were two big defining moments for
us that season, and both involved our quarterback, Len
Dawson. The first was when Lenny hurt his knee in the
second game of the season and wound up missing six
weeks. It was a bad injury, and I remember there was a lot
of talk about if he was going to have surgery or not. As I
recall, Hank [Stram] didn't want him to go under the knife
though, which would cause him to miss the entire season.
So he kept getting second opinions, third opinions, fourth
opinions—until one doctor finally said that Lenny could
probably just avoid surgery altogether and just sit out for
six weeks. That was what Hank wanted to hear, so he went
with it. I'm not sure how Lenny felt, but that was what was
going to be. So, he sat out, and Mike Livingston wound up
filling in for him brilliantly. Even though he was just a
second-year player and very inexperienced, we won six
straight games under his leadership. He wasn't spectacular
by any stretch, but he was solid and just good enough to
win, so I give him a lot of credit.

Lenny eventually came back, and when he did we faced a
pretty big uphill battle. First we had to go out to New York
and face the defending world champion New York Jets.
It was a cold, windy, horrible day in New York, but we
battled and beat those guys 13–6. From there, we headed
out to Oakland to face the Raiders, a team that had
already beaten us twice that year. We battled there as well

in a very tough game and ultimately came out on top after holding them to just seven points, which meant we would be able to represent the AFL in the Super Bowl against the Vikings. So, looking back, if Mike Livingston hadn't stepped up and played liked he did, we never would have had a chance to win it that year.

Lenny was also a factor in another defining moment as well, and this one occurred during the week prior to the Super Bowl. There's always a big news story that week, and this time it was about how Lenny had gotten caught up in an alleged gambling scandal. It became a big distraction; the news media were all over it. It was a nonissue though, nothing. Hank [Stram] called a team meeting a few days before the Super Bowl and announced that a story about Lenny being involved with a known gambler out of Detroit with the same last name was going to be the lead story on the 5:00 news. I remember E.J. Holub stood up and said, 'I don't believe any of that stuff. Lenny has nothing to do with gambling—it's a bunch of B.S. He is one of us and we support him!' We all stood up and cheered and patted Lenny on the back. That was it. We all knew Lenny and knew that there was nothing to it.

Hank was able to use that adversity I think to bring us closer together though. We were already the underdogs coming into the game, and we felt disrespected because of how the NFL tried to make us feel inferior—so this just added fuel to the fire and made us even hungrier to win. It rallied us as a team. It was us against them and made us even more determined. I think it played a big part in us beating Minnesota that day, I really do. I just felt bad for Lenny. He had to answer all the questions with the media and deal with all of that while he was trying to prepare for the game. To his credit though, he was able to focus on what he needed to do that Sunday and get the job done. Lenny was one tough guy. A lot of people didn't realize that his dad also passed away during the season. To be able to overcome all of what he did that season, from start to finish, was pretty remarkable in my opinion."

Jan Stenerud
K, Kansas City Chiefs, 1969

"There were a few that year, starting with Mark Moseley's game-winning field goal against the Giants late in the season. Mark was actually the MVP of the league that year, which was extremely rare. He was so good that year for us though, so clutch; I think he won half of our games that year for us. Another defining moment would be in the NFC Championship Game, when we beat Dallas on our home field at RFK Stadium. We hated the Cowboys and they hated us, and it was the best rivalry in football in those days. I will never forget at the end of the game, after we had sewn it up, the fans were jumping up and down in the stands in unison, and I could literally feel the ground shaking beneath my feet. Just standing there, enjoying that moment, knowing that we were going to the Super Bowl as the ground shook, that was truly a surreal moment that I will never forget. I still get goose bumps thinking about that.

What made that game even extra meaningful for me was the fact that I lost three of my front teeth in it. And it was bad. I went to throw a quick pass, and a guy came up underneath me and caught me in the mouth with his helmet. It hurt like hell, but I didn't miss a play. I didn't want them to think they had hurt me so I just sucked it up. I wore that single-bar face mask, and stuff like that was bound to happen. What are you going to do? Luckily I was able to earn the respect of my teammates and prove to them just how tough I was. I think you lead by example in life. Talk is cheap. You can say all you want, but when you show people that you're willing to lay it all on the line and are willing to take one on the chin, that's when you earn credibility as well as trust.

The other big moment from that season that I will never forget was when I rallied my teammates together just moments before the opening kickoff at the Super Bowl. Nowadays you see guys like Drew Brees getting everybody all fired up, and they all jump up and down together in a big huddle. Well, my big Knute Rockne speech was a little more direct, and the explanation was real simple. I said, 'Guys, this game is worth $72,000 dollars and a big F-ing ring!' That was all I said. Hey, that was a lot of money. My base salary was $235,000 that year, and I was one of the highest-paid guys on the team. So, that bonus check was a significant chunk of change for most of these guys. Needless to say, that was pretty good motivation."

Joe Theismann
QB, Washington Redskins, 1982

"I think that particular team was bigger than any one moment. I think from the minute I got there, it felt like there was something great in the working. There wasn't just one moment I can pinpoint but, rather, a whole bunch of significant moments that all led us down that path toward the Super Bowl. We had success and we had failures along the way, but those are what really refined us to become a championship team. And there were things that happened off the field, as well as on the field, that affected us that season. Certainly the biggest moment of all though was when Tony [Dungy] lost his son [to suicide]—everything changed for us. Our outlook and perspective immediately changed. It was a pivotal time when our team came together and just wrapped each other in love. That right there brought us to a whole new level. As far as things that happened on the field, I would say the biggest moment for us came after we rallied late to beat New England in the AFC Championship Game. We pretty much knew then that winning the Super Bowl was a done deal. We knew that if we could beat those guys in those circumstances, then nothing was going to stand in our way. We played a very tough Bears team in the Super Bowl, but we stayed true to

Colts tight end Ben Utecht carries the ball on an eight-yard reception during the third quarter of Super Bowl XLI. (Doug Pensinger/Getty Images)

our convictions and persevered right up until the end. We beat them 29–17, and I will never forget the feeling of joy I had after the final whistle blew. It was amazing—I was a Super Bowl champion."

Ben Utecht
TE, Indianapolis Colts, 2006

"I remember the New England Patriots had us beat in the first round of the playoffs that year. They were our only loss that season, and we wanted revenge. Well, one of their guys knocked our quarterback, Kenny Stabler, in the head midway through the game on a controversial roughing-the-passer penalty, and as a result we got the ball back. It was just a huge play; they could have ended our season right then and there I think. We got the momentum back and wound up rallying to beat them, 24–21. We had a great fourth quarter. Mark van Eeghan scored late, and then Kenny ran one in from the 1-yard line as well to seal it. Hey, they made a crucial mistake, and the Snake [Stabler] made them pay for it. It was incredible. Those are the kind of things that have to happen when you win the Super Bowl. In addition to having a great team and working hard and all of that, you have to catch a few breaks along the way. From there we beat Pittsburgh in the AFC Championship Game, and then we knocked off the Vikings in the Super Bowl.

There was another defining moment in the Super Bowl as well, and it just so happens that I was a big part of it. I remember there was about five minutes left in the first quarter, and it was still scoreless. We wound up having to punt, so we sent out our punter, Ray Guy. Ray had never gotten a punt blocked in his entire career, and wouldn't you know it, Vikings linebacker Fred McNeill got through and blocked it deep in our end. The ball rolled all the way down to our 3-yard line. Chuck Foreman tried to run it right up the middle on first down, but we stopped him cold. Then, on second down they took out their receivers and brought in a couple of tackles as blockers instead. I had seen this before on film and recognized it right away, so I yelled out, 'Jumbo! Jumbo!' to let my teammates know what was coming. We countered by adding a couple of linebackers, and sure enough, I was able to sneak through and nail Brent McClanahan behind the line of scrimmage. He coughed up the ball, and one of those linebackers, Willie Hall, jumped on it. It was a big momentum swinger for us, and our guys really fed on that. I think it had a big part in our win that day, I really do. We were prepared for what they threw at us, and it was a big feather in our cap that we were able to not only hold them deep in our end, but prevent them from scoring altogether. We drove all the way down the field and scored right after that too, so instead of them getting seven, we got seven. That was huge. We put our game plan to work from there and never looked back. We wound up grinding them down and beating them pretty good, 32–14. We had such a great rhythm that day, nobody could stop us. Minnesota had a great team that year but, hey, that was *our* year."

Phil Villapiano
LB, Oakland Raiders, 1976

"I think every team has that defining game. We had gotten beat 17 straight times by the 49ers—they just owned our division. Well, they came in to our place the fourth week that season, and we destroyed them. It was at that moment where we said to ourselves, 'Hey, we're pretty good. We

can win this whole thing.' For the first time, we really believed in ourselves. That was our defining moment.

I will never forget that final drive [in the Super Bowl]. You know, I had played that game a hundred times in my front yard as a kid; two minutes to go, the ball is in my hands; I throw the touchdown pass to win the Super Bowl. Well, here it was in real life. They had just tied the game up, and I remember going out there for that final drive. Mike [Martz, the offensive coordinator] called a play that we had practiced all week, and we had a very specific way that we wanted to execute it. Sure enough, the defense rotated the way we had hoped that they would, and from there I needed to throw a perfect back-shoulder pass to Isaac Bruce. I remember just as I released it, I got hit by [Titans defensive end] Jevon Kearse and I went down. I saw Isaac catch the ball, but that was all I saw. From there it was just the sound of the crowd going nuts, and that was when I knew that he was going to the house. I didn't get a chance to see it while I was lying on the ground, but I knew that at that point it looked pretty good for us to win the Super Bowl." [5]

Kurt Warner
QB, St. Louis Rams, 1999

Dick Vermeil On Distractions

"As a coach, you have to work on maintaining your focus and try to get the guys to relax a little bit. The families are the big thing; the wives, the kids, the in-laws, the grandparents, they're all coming in for the game, and it can become a distraction. We tried to sequester our guys, to keep them zeroed in on the task at hand. The game is just so big, the magnitude of it, that you really have to keep everybody focused."

CHAPTER
4

Championship Coaches

At the core of every championship team is a great coach. In this chapter I found that every coach had his own method of getting from point A to point B, and no one way was right. What I wanted to find out was how that coach was able to motivate his players that season. What was the secret to his success? Did the players like his style? How was he able to game-plan that season? What was his work ethic like? Did he treat players equally, or did he have different rules for different players? Did he play favorites with the superstars? What was it about him that players were able to grasp on to and buy into? Did he have special "tricks" that he employed to get his players to do certain things? For example, Packers head coach Mike McCarthy had all of his players measured for Super Bowl rings a few days before the big game. Planned or just coincidence? Vision over time equals reality? Hey, it worked. Every coach has a method to his madness. For a coach like Bill Belichick, it was about strategically playing the "disrespect card." Patriot fans remember the video of Belichick, the night before Super Bowl XXXIX, standing in front of his players and showing them the parade route through the city of Brotherly Love that the Eagles had already planned out, presuming victory over his Patriots. Nothing gets a player's blood boiling harder and faster than feeling disrespected. Great coaches can feed on that. They understand which buttons to push for which players, and in this chapter the players talk about what worked for them during that magical season.

TELL ME ABOUT YOUR COACH FROM THAT MAGICAL SEASON.

Vince Lombardi

"Coach Lombardi was a winner. Period. He demanded excellence from his players and just would not tolerate mistakes. He went on and on in practice about execution and fundamentals and about how making mistakes would simply not be acceptable. He preached it every day. It didn't take you very long as a player to figure that out, and as a result, you bought in. He would tolerate physical mistakes, but not mental ones. Dumb penalties, like jumping offside, or committing a turnover, he hated that stuff. He would get after you and ride you until you got better. As a result, our teams were well prepared. That was my big thing with Coach Lombardi, to be mentally prepared in order to do things correctly—both on and off the field. He was a great motivator. He knew when to use the whip and when to use the carrot. That's what made him so unique and so great as a coach in my opinion."

Donny Anderson
RB/P, Green Bay Packers, 1966, 1967

Hank Stram

"Hank had his own philosophies on how the game should be played, and he was a real innovator. The bottom line with Hank though was that he loved to win. We ran a triple-stack defense, with four linebackers lined up, so we did things a little differently. Hank really believed in that system, and we bought into it. He wanted to have his best players all out on the field at the same time together. That was what he wanted to achieve, even if that meant making adjustments throughout the game. He would move guys around; it didn't matter to him. That's why I wound up playing linebacker, even though I had been a tackle and end in college. Hank loved great athletes who were smart players because he figured if you were smart enough and talented enough, it didn't really matter where you played."

Bobby Bell
DE, Kansas City Chiefs, 1969

Weeb Ewbank

"Luckily we had an owner, Carroll Rosenbloom, who wanted to have the best football team in the league. As such, he went out and hired the right person to lead his team, and that was Weeb Ewbank. Weeb was just an offensive line coach under Paul Brown in Cleveland, he had never been a head coach, but Carroll saw something in him and gave him the opportunity. He picked the right guy. Why did we win back-to-back championships in Baltimore? Because we had the right coach in Weeb Ewbank. I think he is one of the top three coaches in the history of the NFL. The reason I say that is because he truly understood the game. His greatest asset in my mind was the fact that he understood the principle of simplicity. He knew that if you had great athletes, that you didn't have to over-burden them with too much stuff. He knew not to give them too many weapons, just enough for them to keep it simple. He didn't overload us with too many plays that were confusing and time consuming. We just focused on what we did best, and that was it. Beyond that, I think he really understood the importance of protecting the quarterback.

As an offensive line coach, he knew how to do that, and as a result, we had a great line, and they were able to give our quarterback, Johnny Unitas, plenty of time to do what he did best—lead. Lastly, I would also say that he understood the balance of running versus passing as well, which was a big deal back in the 1950s. In order to do that, he allowed Unitas to call all the plays—which was pretty amazing when you think about it. He trusted him though, and that was what made those teams so great. He had put an extremely sound system into place, and then he trusted us to run it. Simple, yet profound. The results? Championships. My father was a high school football coach in Texas for 35 years, and I grew up learning the game from him. He and Weeb were very similar in that they both liked to keep things simple. Just sound, funda-mental football, that's it. So, for me it was an easy transi-tion, and I certainly had a lot of respect for the man."

Raymond Berry
WR, Baltimore Colts, 1958, 1959

Bill Cowher

"Bill was a great coach. I think the secret to his success was his ability to step back and get out of the way and just let us do our thing. He did a great job of letting everybody do their job—that was big. He understood the process. He worked hard during the week, and then on Sundays he was able to let go, which put us all at ease."

Jerome Bettis
RB, Pittsburgh Steelers, 2005

Sean Payton

"Sean Payton did a great job of painting the picture for us in that nobody ever remembers who loses the Super Bowl, but you are etched in history for winning it. He said, 'If you lose this game, the confetti comes down, and they are ushering you off the field. The winners, meanwhile, get to stay out there and enjoy it. So let's just make sure we're the ones out there enjoying it when it's all said and done.' That really hit home with us." [1]

Drew Brees
QB, New Orleans Saints, 2009

Lombardi Legacy

The Lombardi Trophy had a special connection to the Saints organization in 2010. Vince Lombardi's grandson, Joe, was the Saints' quarterback coach. "Joe Lombardi, his father Vince Jr., and his two brothers sat and posed with this trophy while pictures were taken," said Saints head coach Sean Payton. "And I just thought to myself, *You have to be kidding me.* If you believe in heaven, and you believe Vince Lombardi's there, looking down on his grandson…this is the guy who coaches our quarterbacks, who coaches Drew Brees. And here's a trophy named after his grandfather. So you can't…you can't get enough of this." [2]

Mike McCarthy

"Coach McCarthy is fantastic. The players really respect him because he's a straight shooter. He talks a lot about the process, about us being true to our brand. He talks about having an identity with the community and about how important that is. Under his leadership, we really feel like we know who we are. He makes the game pretty simple. He just reinforces to us that if we play Green Bay Packer football, then we will have success."

Mason Crosby
K, Green Bay Packers, 2010

Vince Lombardi

"Coach Lombardi was different from anybody who I've ever known. He used fear more and better than anybody I've ever known. He told us that too—he was all business. He told us that he was going to scare us and make us angry. And he said he would keep us angry if necessary so that we could focus and get the job done. While I did not appreciate him while I played for him, I came to appreciate him when I went to see him in his hospital room when he was on his deathbed. It was then that I realized he was demonstrating the same courage there that he had demanded of us on the football field. That validated everything he had done in my eyes, and it really forced me to take another hard look at myself.

Another thing about Coach Lombardi was the fact that he was not prejudiced. You see, most of the teams in the league at that time had quotas for African American players. He did not. He would not tolerate a racist remark at any time. He would not tolerate any divisiveness on the team. He would not tolerate any pejorative names assigned to groups of people. If he heard you say something derogatory about someone, he would kick you off the team so fast you couldn't believe it. As a result, the Herb Adderleys and Willie Davises of the world got along with the Bart Starrs and Jimmy Taylors. Those leaders, black and white, they then set an example for the rest of us. That

Packers players carry coach Vince Lombardi off the field after the Packers defeated the Oakland Raiders 33–14 in Super Bowl II. (AP Images)

created cohesiveness amongst us, chemistry, if you will. Yes, we had great players in those days—but so did other teams. What made us special and unique was that cohesiveness that we shared. That was Coach Lombardi's gift. As tough as he was, he was able to bring us together and play like a team. That's why we won championships under his leadership in my opinion."

Bill Curry

C, Green Bay Packers, 1965, 1966; Baltimore Colts, 1970

Vince Lombardi

"Coach Lombardi motivated through fear; that was how he got us to be our best. Winning was the easy way out with him, because you were only going to get a small amount of criticism. Losing, however, that was a whole other story. You just did not want to disappoint him. He was demanding and expected a lot out of us, but he was fair and got results. We knew that if we followed his leadership, he would bring us to the promised land, and by gosh he did. He was a good man."

Willie Davis
DE, Green Bay Packers,
1961, 1962, 1965, 1966, 1967

Mike Ditka

"If I had to describe one thing about my style as a coach, I would say it's 'I am who I am.' I can't change who I am. I didn't try to fool them, and I didn't try to bullshit them either. So, what they saw was what they got. Look, as a coach, I hammered home results. I always figured that if you do the right things, you get the right results. You gotta treat people with respect too, that's the key. You can't treat everybody the same either. You had the same rules for everybody, but you gotta handle people differently. Some people you gotta coddle, others you gotta be stern with. Once you were able to figure that out, then it was all downhill from there. Once you got your guys to buy into what you were selling, that was when coaching became less of a job and more about fun. Because when you're having fun, you're winning—and that's the name of the game in this business."

Mike Ditka
TE, Dallas Cowboys, 1971;
Head Coach, Chicago Bears, 1985

Weeb Ewbank

"Weeb was a really smart guy. There is no smarter coach in the NFL today than Weeb was back then. He knew it all. He was like a school teacher, always working with us and trying to help us get better. I had a lot of respect for the guy, I really did."

Art Donovan
DT, Baltimore Colts, 1958, 1959

Bill Walsh

"Everybody played as a team within the organization—Bill made sure of it. He ran that team like a business; it was very businesslike in the way he did things. He was an amazing coach, no question. With Bill it was all about respect. You didn't celebrate after a sack or a big tackle, that kind of stuff was frowned upon. The only guy who got away with it was Jerry [Rice], who would do the 'Cabbage Patch' [celebration] once in a while after he scored a big touchdown. Bill would let that go because, hey, it was Jerry Rice after all. Bill used to motivate guys by making sure that they appreciated their jobs. He welcomed competition at every position because he knew that would keep guys working hard at all times.

You always felt like you were on the bubble. You were never that comfortable with your job security, and that was by design. He just made you feel unsure, questioning everything about what you did in the previous game and what you were about to do in the next game. They liked to give guys one-year contracts, to keep you hungry, knowing you could always be let go. They weren't afraid to cut you either, to make a point. In fact, I was cut three different times by the Niners. The first time Bill cut me it was for one week. He wanted to make sure I learned that this was a business. I didn't hear that from Bill himself, mind you, I heard it from a reporter who told me about it. Needless to say, I learned my lesson. I came back a week later ready to work hard and do whatever I was told.

I remember after losing a couple of bad games during the '88 season coming back to the locker room after the game. There was a big refrigerator with glass doors in there, and one of them had a huge hole in it from somebody's foot. We all knew at that point that Eddie DeBartolo had been there and that he obviously wasn't very happy. We all just went, 'Oh my God!' The way I felt was that, okay, I had better step up my game big time, otherwise I am going to be playing for somebody else next season. I knew I had to play my butt off, otherwise there were going to be consequences. It was a big wake-up call to all of us that we needed to get our shit together in a hurry. Needless to say, we wound up winning every game after that right on through the Super Bowl. So, they sort of had these veiled threats, if you will, where they don't even really have to say anything at all. You just knew, and as a result, you did not want to disappoint the organization. There were probably five or six guys who were untouchable, the Montanas and the Rices, the superstars, but beyond that nobody ever really felt like their job was safe. Hey, that was great motivation. It worked.

The Niners paid us a little bit more than most teams too, which was also an added motivation. It was a perk. A lot of players wanted to play for the Niners. They just had this aura about them, a mystique, that trickled down from the ownership group to the coaching staff. They were *the* marquee team of that era, much like the Yankees are in

San Francisco 49ers coach Bill Walsh gets a lift on the shoulders of his players after Super Bowl XIX. San Francisco topped Miami 38–16 at Stanford Stadium. (AP Images)

baseball. They just did things bigger and better than everybody else. So, overall it was a great experience, but it was also very stressful. They did things differently though, and that was why they were so successful for so many years.

Jim Fahnhorst
LB, San Francisco 49ers,
1984, 1988, 1989

Bill Walsh On His Final Game—Super Bowl XXIII

"We finally got back to the Super Bowl in 1989, and that was an outstanding team that was also a hard-luck team.… We had a tough time in Super Bowl XXIII [vs. Cincinnati], sort of bumbling along during the game, self-destructing until we had to win it. We just had a tough time with them. We made over 400 yards on offense and still weren't scoring. It took a three-minute drive ['The Drive'] at the end of the game going the length of the field to finally win it. It was our job to move 92 yards down the field and execute.

The drive itself was a culmination of 10 years as head coach of the San Francisco 49ers. I just feel so fortunate that the last drive related to teamwork, execution, poise, and confidence. There was never a thought of 'Let's go for it all and hit Jerry [Rice] on a long one.' No. It was execution. There isn't anything verbal that had to be said. I didn't have to say, 'Men, this is very important.' I had a game plan and knew that Joe [Montana] believed in it and could execute it. I couldn't think of emotion. I couldn't think of the gravity of it or the importance of it. My job was to function under the tremendous stress. Following the play [when Montana hit John Taylor on a 10-yard game-winning touchdown], I told my staff that we had just run the perfect play to win the world championship. It was a play that basically I designed out of nowhere, so I was really proud of myself, feeling that this perfect play was the last play of my NFL coaching career…only to find later that our running backs had in fact lined up all wrong and run the patterns the opposite way. Oh boy." [3]

Bill Walsh

"Bill was a master motivator as well as a master manipulator. He just had this way of making you feel insecure about your job that always kept you on edge. He did it to everybody too, even Joe [Montana]. He was always playing mind games with Joe because he knew that was how he could motivate him. Bill's gift though was to realize which guys he could do that with and which ones needed to be coddled. Some guys would just lose all of their self-confidence and crumble in those situations. So, he knew which buttons to push with which people in order to get them to play harder. He messed with me all the time—I was used to it. He always thought I was too small and wanted me to get bigger. So he would talk about how the team really needed a big [offensive] tackle. Stuff like that; he would just throw stuff out there in front of everyone, and you knew who he was talking to. That was just his way of kind of needling you. As players, we didn't always realize it at the time, but he was motivating us in his own way. We weren't really happy about it, but that was his M.O. You just had to accept the fact that yes, there was a method to his madness, and it ultimately paid off in the end because we were able to win championships."

Keith Fahnhorst
OT, San Francisco 49ers, 1981, 1984

Tom Coughlin

"Coach Coughlin was a no-nonsense kind of a guy. He was by the book. He was really a stickler for the details. He was punctual and very demanding. If you didn't follow the rules, then there were going to be consequences. He was not afraid to call you out and discipline you. That was his style. He was a team guy and just had his own way of going about his business. Hey, you certainly can't argue with the results. The guy is a great coach."

Marcus Freeman
TE, New York Giants, 2007

Hank Stram

"Hank was always prepared. He had a game plan every week, and we stuck to it. We knew as players that as long as we executed that game plan, then we would have no problem winning. So that gave us a lot of confidence. Hank was also very good at evaluating personnel, just a great judge of talent. In those days you could find guys in the later rounds of the draft or via free agency that were under the radar, whereas today with all of the media coverage that would be impossible. Hank was always really good about finding and developing those guys. He was just a really good coach. We believed in him and wanted to win for him."

Mike Garrett
RB, Kansas City Chiefs, 1969

Tom Landry

"Playing for Coach Landry really gave you a solid foundation for life after football because he was all business when it came to the Dallas Cowboys. He set goals for us and then held us accountable to those goals. He would tell us, 'If you do this, then we will win.' In fact, I think Coach Landry had more to do with my success in business than anybody else. The way he ran the team was just like a CEO. He wasn't one of the guys who would scream and holler, like Lombardi. He was more reserved—strictly business. If you did things his way, then usually the play worked. And if you didn't run the play his way, then usually it didn't work. He was very methodical and liked to set up game plans for us. Not only was he a great coach, he was a great man."

Walt Garrison
RB, Dallas Cowboys, 1971

Vince Lombardi

"Being around Coach Lombardi, you always wanted to strive to do your best; he just brought that out of all of us. There was only one place for him, and that was first place. That meant that you had to apply your best effort to everything. He was all business, no doubt about it. He was so intense and enthusiastic; you just couldn't help having that rub off on you when you were around the guy. You almost had to be a part of that because if you weren't, or couldn't, then you were gone pretty quickly. That's just how it was in those days. He picked players who thought like he did and who were full of energy and enthusiasm and could really get after it, and that was why he was so successful."

Gale Gillingham
G, Green Bay Packers, 1966, 1967

Vince Lombardi

"I learned so much from Vince. He was such a great coach and such a good man. As a coach, he demanded a lot from us; he expected a lot from us; and eventually we got to the point where we simply did not want to disappoint him. He worked us hard, real hard, but we always knew that he was going to work even harder in putting together an effective game plan that would give us the best chance to win. The guy was just a winner. Period."

Forrest Gregg
OT, Green Bay Packers,
1961, 1962, 1965, 1966, 1967

Chuck Noll

"Chuck was very businesslike. It was as if he was the CEO of a corporation. We all bought into that. He was big on preparation, from training camp on through the season. Every week he had a game plan, and we followed it. He was very disciplined. He knew what it took to become a championship football team and demanded excellence from every one of us. I think that Chuck learned a lot when he was an assistant under Don Shula in Baltimore. They lost to Joe Namath and the Jets in Super Bowl III, and I think that really motivated him. He wanted to win it. From that I think he learned that yes, the Super Bowl is a big game, but don't make it bigger than life. As such, he tried to run our practice schedules with a great deal of consistency. He didn't try to overcoach us or overprepare us, which was a big reason why he was 4–0 in his Super Bowls. He was just a very good coach, one of the best of all time."

Jack Ham
LB, Pittsburgh Steelers,
1974, 1975, 1978, 1979

Tom Flores

"Tom was a great coach, but because we had so many great leaders on that team, we didn't really need a whole lot of extra motivation. Our motivation as players was to win the Super Bowl, and Tom understood that. He wasn't a real rah-rah guy; he was more laid back and relaxed. As players, we fed off of that energy—he kept us grounded. We had a lot of distractions that season, but Tom was able to keep us focused on the task at hand. That brought us together too and just added to the cama-raderie. In addition to Tom doing his thing, we also had

Al Davis around every day as well. Not many teams have their owner at practice, looking in on the day-to-day stuff, but that was how it was with the Raiders. He was very hands-on. So, he and Tom were out there, and it was cool. We were one united team from the top down. As such, everybody shared in the wins and the losses. It was a big family. It was a unique organization; a lot of tradition and history."

Mike Haynes
CB, Los Angeles Raiders, 1983

Don McCafferty

"Don had been the team's offensive coordinator under Don Shula prior to taking over as the head coach that season, and all of the players really respected him. For him to win it in his first season was pretty incredible. Don was a good coach, and he treated everybody fairly. He was tough though. When you stepped out of line, you knew the consequences. He wasn't a big motivational speaker or anything like that; he was more quiet and reserved. He left it up to us to motivate ourselves, which was unique. The players loved him though and played hard for him. After winning the Super Bowl in '71, we wound up losing to Shula's Dolphins in the AFC Championship Game [the following season]. It was a really tight game, and it came down to Paul Warfield's big catches that put them over the top. We never recovered from it for whatever reason, and the next season we started out pretty bad. I will never forget that next season when we were just 1–4, and our general manager told Don to bench our quarterback, Johnny Unitas. Don refused and got fired. It was pretty intense, and we almost had a mutiny. I remember all of us players getting together and basically refusing to play that next week unless they gave Don his job back. Coach Sandusky took over and talked us into playing, which we did, but we were all really upset. Don went on to coach the Lions, but sadly he died of a heart attack just a couple years later. It was really sad—he was a good man."

Ted Hendricks
LB, Baltimore Colts, 1970;
Oakland Raiders, 1976, 1980;
Los Angeles Raiders, 1983

John Madden
"What you saw was what you got with John. He was just always full of energy, and his personality was almost larger than life. John was a motivator and loved to get us all fired up. He knew when to yell and scream at you and when to praise you and pat you on the back. He was a player's coach, and we wanted to win for him. Great guy, heck of a coach."

Ted Hendricks
LB, Baltimore Colts, 1970;
Oakland Raiders, 1976, 1980;
Los Angeles Raiders, 1983

Tom Flores
"Tom was a very good football coach. He wasn't a yeller and a screamer; he was very quiet and conservative. The players played for him. What Tom will always be remembered for was how he revived Jim Plunkett's career. Jim had been a great quarterback up in New England, but as the years went on his game floundered a little bit. So, when he came to the Raiders, he was revitalized and really

stepped up his game. Tom was able to work with him, and those two just had a great connection."

Ted Hendricks
LB, Baltimore Colts, 1970;
Oakland Raiders, 1976, 1980;
Los Angeles Raiders, 1983

Joe Gibbs

"Coach Gibbs was a great administrator of his staff. He had a veteran staff who had been with him for a long time, and he trusted them to do their jobs, guys like Charley Taylor, Emmitt Thomas, Richie Petitbon. They were all former players and had a great chemistry together. They were real professionals. They were very loyal to Joe, and he rewarded them by allowing them to have very long leashes. He didn't micromanage them; he just let them do their thing—which I thought was very unique. Coach Gibbs was a man of few words, but you knew it when he was hot or upset. He was a great motivator. He didn't get upset very often, but when he did he would do so at just the right time to really make a point. He let the players get after it too—we had fights in practice pretty regularly. He wanted everybody to play with an edge. You had to be hungry and willing to go all out for him; he was demanding in that sense. Guys responded well to him though and wanted to please him. He was a good Christian, he was fair, and he was a straight shooter. He was just an amazing coach, one of the best ever."

Ray Hitchcock
G, Washington Redskins, 1987

Vince Lombardi

"To be honest, I didn't enjoy myself my first couple of years in Green Bay with the coaching staff that we had up there. I didn't agree with much of what they did, and it was a tough situation for me. Guys were just running around loose as a goose, and I was never used to that kind of thing. I was used to discipline at Notre Dame. Their philosophy was to win at all times, and that was why they had a successful program. Well, when I got to Green Bay, it seemed like everyone was playing for themselves, for their own contracts. I was totally disgusted by it all to tell you the truth, almost to the point where I was ready to just give it up. No kidding. Luckily though, that was when Lombardi came to town, and with him came a whole new sense of purpose. He changed everything, and in the process he made football fun again. When Lombardi got to Green Bay, he changed our whole thinking about competing. We finally understood what it was to win under Lombardi. When you get a coach you really like and admire, and you know that he knows what the hell he's doing—you trust him—that's when you are going to give it your all, and you're going to see some positive results. It took us about a year to learn his system, and after that we were off to the races. Once we had it down, we were a pretty tough team to beat."

Paul Hornung
HB, Green Bay Packers,
1961, 1962, 1965, 1966

Mike McCarthy

"Coach McCarthy's really a player's coach. He tries hard to take care of us. He takes the time to get to know the players, so we respect him. He really makes sure that everything stays fun, too, and that it's not all business.

Practices are never dull. He mixes it up and gives us lots of different activities—which goes a long way with the players. As players, we just really like him and his style. He's pretty low key, not too loud and not too quiet—just right. He's just a great coach; we're lucky to have him."

Cullen Jenkins
DE, Green Bay Packers, 2010

Bill Walsh

"From an Xs and Os perspective, he was the brightest coach that has ever lived. He could predict things before they would even happen. He could draw things up on paper and know exactly how the defense was going to react to it. He saw the game on a higher level. The complexity at which he ran that offense and what he demanded of his players to execute, it was unparalleled in history. So you had this sophisticated 'genius' side of Bill, but you also had this equally magnificent side of him, which doesn't get as much credit, the motivational side. Bill did not treat everybody equally. That, in my opinion, was his greatest gift. He treated everybody with respect, but he understood that different guys had different personalities. With 50 different characters in the locker room, from all walks of life and backgrounds, Bill knew that each player had his own unique way of being motivated. Some guys were motivated by fame. Some guys were motivated by money. Some guys were motivated by the threat of losing their jobs. Some guys were motivated by being yelled at. Some guys were motivated by a pat on the back.

Bill realized, as a great manager, leader, and CEO, that his players were all driven to succeed with different motivations. As such, he was a master at figuring out what made each player tick. He would spend time with guys and study them. Then, once he knew, he would use those motivational techniques to get the most out of that guy. Bill also knew that once guys were motivated and driven, however, that the battle was going to be in keeping them motivated and driven. To do that, everybody had a quality backup at their position who would push them. He always wanted his starters to feel uncomfortable about their role. Bill would just have to casually say, 'Hey, if you're not getting it done, then your backup will.' And that was all it took. Everybody had that pressure on them, and it drove us all nuts. Joe Montana was the only guy who never really had a 'threatening' backup, so Bill went out and traded for Steve Young. Once Steve came on board, he pushed Joe and he pushed him hard. And it worked, because I would argue that Joe's best years as a 49er, the late '80s, were when Steve was pushing him. He pushed him to be even greater than he already was, which is pretty amazing when you think about it. That was Bill's master plan, and it was purely genius.

Bill's philosophy was encapsulated into what we called the '49er Way.' Prior to him coming here, the Niners were a pretty rag-tag organization and relatively unsuccessful for most of their history. Trust me, having grown up in the Bay Area, I can tell you that it was not an organization that you associated with success. Well, Bill changed the culture here. The 49er Way started with the way you conducted yourself both on and off the field. Off the field, you had to do your homework and study hard. Bill brought in highly sophisticated and bright players because the schemes that we ran were very complicated. You had to be able to react and understand and be capable of taking in extraordinary amounts of detailed and highly complex information. On the field, we did things with a purpose. Everything ran like clockwork according to Bill's schedule. We ran from drill to drill—we didn't walk with our helmets off. As a receiver, we caught balls and then sprinted 40 yards downfield; we wouldn't just jog five yards or slow down. That manifested itself in games where you saw our receivers catching short slant routes and then busting a tackle and sprinting 60 yards for a touchdown. Bill believed that you practiced the way you played. He never had us practice in pads very often because he wanted us to be fresh come December and playoff time. We practiced full speed, at a super high tempo, but he wanted us to be healthy.

The 49er Way was also about how we traveled as a team. We got to our destinations a day early to get acclimated. Guys had their own hotel rooms. We flew in DC-10s versus 737s, and we had catered food on board. Everything was first class all the way. Being a West Coast team, we really prepared for East Coast trips differently. We had a structure to it, a plan—it wasn't just another trip. Our owner, Eddie DeBartolo, completely bought into that as well and would spend whatever it took to keep us happy and also give us an advantage. I'm sure that probably cost a couple hundred thousand dollars to do that, but he felt like it was worth it. With the Niners, it wasn't about winning the conference championship or making the playoffs. Everybody in that entire organization was 100 percent committed to winning the Super Bowl every single year. High goals, high ideals, and high expectations. That attitude and state of mind just permeated the entire organization. Guys who didn't work hard or who were self-promoters, they didn't fit in. They stood out drastically and were never around for very long.

When I think of Bill's legacy, I can see that it's alive and well today in the NFL. Every coach who came from the Bill Walsh 'tree,' every one whether they admit it or not, took the 49er Way with them to their new teams. Mike Holmgren turned the Green Bay Packers into 49ers-Wisconsin. He turned that team around with these exact same philosophies. Mike Shanahan turned the Denver Broncos into 49ers–Colorado. He won back-to-back Super Bowls in the late '90s using this system. Mike used to spend hours and hours with Bill, just soaking it all in like a sponge. Bill was so generous with his time and would share his ideas; that was just his personality. Then, you take it a step further and think about Mike Holmgren's tree, with guys like Steve Mariucci and Andy Reid [both head coaches]. They have carried on that attitude of excellence too. So it's far reaching and pretty profound to think about. Bill was just such a great man, absolutely brilliant, and he left us far too soon. I miss him."

Brent Jones
TE, San Francisco 49ers,
1988, 1989, 1994

Tom Landry
"Tom taught leadership by example. He didn't just talk about it, he actually did it. He was very hands-on in that regard, and that was what made him so unique I think. He was a very challenging person. He demanded a lot out of his players and expected a lot. He was very committed and dedicated to his players though. He told you what you needed to bring to the table every single day and held you accountable to that. He knew what it took to be successful and was not afraid to call guys out if he thought that they weren't pulling their weight. He did it in a very businesslike manner, very respectfully, but he made it clear in no uncertain terms if he felt like you were not performing at a high level. He just made sure that we knew that unless we were

all willing to work at an extremely high level, then we
shouldn't expect to win a championship. Sure enough, the
year we won it, we were all playing at that level—due in
large part to Tom's coaching and motivational style."

Lee Roy Jordan
LB, Dallas Cowboys, 1971

Don Shula

"Don motivated through intimidation. You realized that if you
were a warrior, a veteran, then you didn't mind doing all the
things that this maniac demanded that you do. If you were
worth your salt, you didn't mind. You just did them, knowing
that once you did, then good things were invariably going to
happen. He was right there with us too; he worked his ass
off right alongside of us. He demanded everything that we
had, but he also gave it to us first. That was what made him
such a good coach and so well respected in my opinion; he
wasn't afraid to lead by example."

Bob Kuechenberg
OL, Miami Dolphins, 1972, 1973

Don Shula

"We had great leadership at the top. Don was an extraordinary coach, and it was certainly a privilege to play for
him. I played for 10 seasons under him and feel very fortunate to have done so. Don was an intense guy. His practices were intense too; there was nothing half-assed about
them. He was 100 percent geared toward winning, every
single day. That was his focus. He worked extremely hard.
There were a lot of early mornings and late nights for the
guy, almost a 24-hour-a-day job when you think about it.
He never got away from the game—it consumed him. He

was just very focused. I remember sitting in the film room one time, and he ran a single play back 60–70 times. He absolutely demanded excellence. The film didn't lie; if he saw something, he pointed it out and got after you. If it was a mental mistake, he didn't want it to happen again. He was very vocal. He was very consistent, year in and year out. And he set a standard of excellence for his players that he held us accountable to. He was relentless in how he drove us. You went all out on every down, or you were going to hear about it from him. That was his philosophy for success, and it worked.

Don was all business when it came to football. I remember we were about to scrimmage another team during training camp one year, and he came up to me right before it was about to start. He said, 'Jim, I just got word that your dad passed away. I'm very sorry. But we need you for this practice.' I was pretty shaken up, but I didn't want to let the team down so of course I suited up. Then, afterward, he came up to me and said, 'Jim, we'll get you a plane ticket so you can go back home to Minnesota for the funeral. We'll see you back here in a couple of days for practice. Please give our condolences to your family.' I couldn't believe it! Hey, looking back, I totally understand it. He was running a business and needed me. I was the starting center on the team, and we didn't have a bunch of backups or anything in those days. He expected us to act like professionals at all times, and I'm sure in his eyes he felt like he was being more than gracious by getting me a ticket to go home for a couple of days to attend the funeral.

Don was a throwback. In fact, I don't know how Don would do as a coach in today's game to tell you the truth. I'm not sure how his motivational tactics would work on a guy who was making $20 million a season. How crazy is that? Back then some guys were making 25 grand a season, and they were just happy to have a job. The winner's share of the Super Bowl was 15 grand, which was a lot of money in those days. Motivation aside, that was a pretty big incentive for some guys. So, it's a totally different world today than it was back then, that's for sure. Don was a heckuva coach though, and we wanted to win for him. He was a very credible person, and we trusted him and believed in him. He was a winner in every sense of the word, and I'm proud to have played for him."

Jim Langer
C, Miami Dolphins, 1972, 1973

Tom Landry
"Coach Landry wasn't like Vince Lombardi or any of those 'motivational' types of coaches. He was more subdued. He wasn't flashy, just steady. Consistent. He was a goal setter; that was very important to him. He had a plan, and we were going to follow that plan. His motivation was for us to set goals in training camp and then work hard on accomplishing those goals throughout the season. He knew that if we did that, then we were going to be successful. We set goals, all of us, and then tracked our progress all season long. He was very detail oriented in that way, but the results didn't lie.

We also worked on the fundamentals a lot each year too; that was very important to him. We watched a lot of film and worked on our techniques. We scrimmaged a lot as well, because he was always evaluating us and wanted to see our progress on a regular basis. Coach Landry was consistent; he had great integrity and character; he was honest; he cared for us; and he was just an overall really smart guy. Brilliant. He worked us hard and was demanding, yet he

Cowboys coach Tom Landry takes the field during warmups prior to Super Bowl VI. Landry's Cowboys played in five Super Bowls, winning two, during the 1970s. (AP Images)

was well respected by his players. We trusted him. He was also an extraordinary evaluator of talent. He liked smart players, to get guys on his teams who could think and who could comprehend and execute his game plans. It wasn't surprising to see him have great success in his life after football either, because all of those characteristics applied directly to business. He was an extraordinary businessman.

Interestingly, even though he was very caring toward his players, he wasn't real close to them like some coaches are. He was more distant. Afterward, however, he would be the most friendly person in the world and just love you dearly. I remember asking about why he wasn't friendly with us while we were playing, and he said, 'Well, I'm the guy who has to fire you and tell you when you're over the hill, which is not a very easy thing to do to your friend.' So while outside his persona was more distant, inside he was a very tender man."

Bob Lilly
DT, Dallas Cowboys, 1971

Joe Gibbs

"Coach Gibbs was a phenomenal coach. He was a hard worker and really led by example. He did so much prep work and game planning. He spent most of his time at the practice facility. He was just consumed with getting us ready and prepared, both mentally and physically. A lot of the credit for our success goes to him; he was our leader, and we all really respected him. He knew how to motivate us. He didn't have to say too much either; he was just straight and to the point. He wasn't a screamer or yeller—he just spoke to you like a professional. The bottom line with Coach Gibbs was that he was a winner. The guy knew how to win, plain and simple."

Chip Lohmiller
K, Washington Redskins, 1990

Weeb Ewbank

"Weeb's biggest asset was the fact that he was a great judge of talent. He did his homework and could recruit guys like crazy. He was a smart guy. As an offensive-minded coach, he was very innovative too. I remember when he took our great running back, Lenny Moore, out of the backfield and put him out as a flanker. Nowadays you see that all the time, but in the '50s it was unheard of.

Weeb's downfall was the fact that he was probably too nice of a guy. The players liked him, but eventually he couldn't control the team. You can't be pals with your players—it just doesn't work. They won't respect you the way that you need to be respected in order to win."

Gino Marchetti
DE, Baltimore Colts, 1958, 1959

Bill Parcells
"Bill was a great coach; the guys played for him because they respected him. He was tough but fair. He just knew what buttons to push for which guys and when to push them. The one thing that I loved about the guy was that he made me grow up real quick. He taught me responsibility and forced me to become accountable. That was something I needed early in my career, and I appreciate what he did for me."

Leonard Marshall
DE, New York Giants, 1986, 1990

Tony Dungy
"Tony and I go back a long way. I helped recruit him and coached him back at the University of Minnesota in the '70s, so our friendship runs deep. We both learned the majority of our football under Chuck Noll, with the Pittsburgh Steelers. The man can coach, no doubt about it. The players respect him and genuinely like him. Tony's just a special person. He's very intelligent. He's very calm. He's very consistent. He has a great demeanor. He's a great coach, but he's also a great person."

Tom Moore
Offensive Coordinator, Indianapolis Colts, 2006

Don Shula

"Coach Shula ran a tight ship. He was a planner. He had game plans for everything and followed through with them. He made sure we were accountable to them as well. He wouldn't tolerate guys goofing around or any of that stuff either—he was tough. When we got out on the field, he was all business. We had two practice fields down in Miami, side by side, and somehow he knew exactly what everybody was doing on both fields at the same time. I think he had eyes in the back of his head because he was always aware of what was happening around him. He didn't miss a thing; if you were loafing off or taking a breather, he would scream across the field at you to get back to work. It was amazing. He demanded your full attention, your complete focus, and he expected you to give your very best. You did it the right way or you were going to do it again and again and again. That was why he was so successful; he just wouldn't tolerate anything other than your best effort. As long as you worked hard and gave it your all, he was right there with you. You had his support. If you weren't willing to go all out day in and day out, then you probably weren't going to be around for very long. You may not have liked everything he did or the way he went about doing it, but you certainly respected him. He was just a great, great coach."

Earl Morrall

QB, Baltimore Colts, 1970;
Miami Dolphins, 1972, 1973

Weeb Ewbank

"Weeb was a good coach. He was a good organizer and liked to put game plans together for us. He'd get nervous on game day, but that excitement kind of got us going a little bit too—we fed off his energy. He only had a handful of assistant coaches in those days too, not like today where teams have 15 assistants out there helping out. So, he had to do a lot of work and was very thorough about it. He worked hard and was committed to doing whatever it took for us to win ballgames. I loved him; I'd run through a brick wall for him. He was a good man."

Andy Nelson
CB, Baltimore Colts, 1958, 1959

Tom Flores

"Tom was a player's coach. He put it all out there for us, what we needed to do, and he expected us to do our jobs. He wasn't a rah-rah guy or anything like that. He delegated a lot of authority to his assistant coaches too, which was unique. He hired people whom he respected and trusted to do their jobs, and then he let them do their jobs."

Bob Nelson
DT, Oakland Raiders, 1980;
Los Angeles Raiders, 1983

Bill Parcells

"Bill was a guy who motivated through fear. He was tough. If you didn't do it his way, then there were going to be consequences. He was very good at getting key people to buy into his philosophies though. He knew that if he could get certain guys to be on board with him then everybody else would follow—guys like Lawrence Taylor and Harry Carson, who were really respected veterans. He was just really good at tapping into certain people and utilizing them to get his point across. Bill's philosophy was that you ran the football and you stop the run. Period. So, we ran the football. And when that didn't work, we ran the football some more. As a wide receiver, that was frustrating at times, but that was the game plan, and that was how he wanted to go to battle. We had to make plays when it was our time. We had to take advantage of those rare situations where our number got called. He was a great coach; players responded to him and wanted to please him. The guy was a winner."

Stacy Robinson
WR, New York Giants, 1986, 1990

Mike McCarthy

"Mike doesn't like to hear this, but he's a player's coach. He thinks there's a negative connotation there. To me, it means he allows for input from his guys on a number of different levels, and obviously he has final say, but he allows his staff to coach, he allows the players to have input. He has final veto power obviously, and I think that his greatest quality is he allows input in the schedule, input in the way we do things. And I think he's really set up a schedule, a team, a program that allows his players to be successful and his coaches to coach, and he's assembled an incredible staff and a lot of high-character guys. I have to give credit to [General Manager] Ted [Thompson] and Mike on putting this team together, but also to Mike for allowing his coaches to coach and his players to play."[4]

Aaron Rodgers
QB, Green Bay Packers, 2010

Mike McCarthy On His Approach Leading Up to Super Bowl XLV

"I did a couple of things differently down the stretch. The playoff captains speaking to the team before the game, that just popped in my head. I was thinking about it driving home one night and prayed on it. I didn't know if that was the right thing to do.... There was a positive response that came from that. It was risky for the head coach to give up the final message to his team before he goes out onto the field. You've just got to trust your instincts.

I am not perfect, but the one thing I think the players truly know that they get from me, they get the truth and it comes from the heart. They know it is researched. They know our staff is very detail oriented. We don't ever walk into a meeting unprepared. We don't just try new things because so-and-so did it last week in the game, and I think they respect that from us. There is a belief in how we operate, and that was the biggest key for us down the stretch. We were a consistent football team all year. I never felt we were as bad as our record may have been sometimes or as good as when we had the blowout win. We were just a very consistent football team, and that is why we ended up being the Super Bowl champions." [5]

Don Shula

"I worked for Don for nine years, so I got to know him as good as anybody I suppose. Don was such a great coach, one of the all-time greats in this game without a doubt. He was a real visionary. I think the reason Don was able to keep it all together that season was because he approached every game—from the opening game to the last game to the first playoff game to the Super Bowl—with the same degree of preparation. He had a real businesslike determination to him. He had a very strong work ethic too. He liked to keep his guys on very consistent schedules, us assistant coaches included. During the first week of June, that was when we broke down film and made training reels. Every year, that was what we did, at the exact same time. If it was Tuesday night at 10 o'clock and the entire coaching staff was all out to dinner together, that meant we had just finished making our game plans for the upcoming Sunday. At training camp, everything ran like clockwork; that was how Don liked to do things. He was a creature of habit without a doubt. He was just very professional and very consistent in everything he did. There was a definite method to his madness. The players not only respected Don, they liked him as well—and that says a lot in my opinion. Don is a very religious person too. He attended Catholic schools all the way through college, and his faith is very important to him. Back when he was coaching he used to go to church every single morning. So, that was obviously very important to him. He's just an incredible person, and I'm very proud to have had the opportunity to work with him. He's a good man."

Howard Schnellenberger
Assistant Coach, Miami Dolphins, 1972

Mike Ditka

"Mike was a great coach. In terms of the passion that he had for the game, I would say that my coaching style is a lot like his. He really, really loved football. That wasn't something that he told you, you just saw it. And he knew the game so well; he truly was a student of the game. He had a vision, he had a passion, and he had a supporting cast. The organization was behind him too. When I think about the keys to his success, one of the big things is the fact that he had a general manager who was one of his best friends. When you have that kind of camaraderie and trust, and you can say, 'Hey, I need you to go get this player...' and it gets done, and you don't have to worry about agendas or motives. That's huge. Lastly, he had the personnel that believed in him, guys like me, Dan Hampton, Walter Payton, Steve McMichael, Fridge, and on and on—we supported him. So, when you have all of those things in place, from the top down, it's going to be hard to fail."

Mike Singletary
LB, Chicago Bears, 1985

Mike Tomlin

"Coach Tomlin's just a no-nonsense guy. You always know where you stand with him, good or bad. If you're not play-ing well, he'll tell you. He's a very smart person. He studies hard and works hard. That attitude really trickles down to the players too; we certainly feed on his lead-by-example attitude. He doesn't say a whole either, but what he does say he really means. When he talks, he commands the whole attention of the entire room. I don't know how he does it, but he just always says the right thing at the right time. He's steady, not too many highs and not too many lows. He never worries about how we're going to react after a loss because he knows we don't like losing. He doesn't just yell at us to punish us. He knows that after we lose that everybody's going to work extra hard in practice so that we can get back on the winning track. He's a player's coach; we respect him and want to win for him."

Matt Spaeth
TE, Pittsburgh Steelers, 2008

Jon Gruden On Winning Super Bowl XXXVII with Tampa

"Winning the Super Bowl, that was the most exciting day of my life. I'll never forget it. You want to share it with the guys you work with. We rejoiced after that game, together. Whether you're getting Gatorade showers or whether you're jumping up and down hugging people, grown men, that's what this game is all about. That's why you go to training camp. That's why you work hard. If you can win one of these games, it just makes it all worthwhile. We worked so hard, and so many guys sacrificed so much to have success and win. Don't ever underestimate the great thrill behind victory. Winning is what you remember. It's the most important thing. It's not the only thing though; it's also the relationships along the way. I really enjoy some of the relationships that I have been able to create with the players; some of them are long lasting. Those are the things that I'll remember the most." [6]

Vince Lombardi

"We had some great teams in those days in Green Bay, and the leader of those teams was Vince Lombardi, the greatest coach of all time in my opinion. Coach Lombardi led by example, as well as through example. You see, he was all about teaching the basics and the fundamentals, and he was a wonderful living example of that. His life was prioritized, and it went in this order: 1) God, 2) Family, and 3) Others. And oh, by the way, we, the Green Bay Packers, were the Others. He had his priorities straight and devoted himself to those three things. When you are that devoted, and that prioritized, then you are going to strive every day to be the very best that you can be. When you were around him, you could just sense that this man wanted to be the very best that he could be.

When he first came to the Packers, there was no offensive coordinator. He was the head coach as well as the offensive coordinator. I used to love going to his team meetings because I couldn't wait to start taking notes on whatever he was commenting about that day. Not only was he a great coach, but he was also an outstanding teacher, and that was something he was extremely proud of. He was such a smart man. It was so exciting to watch him break down film and to see the way he did it, so methodically and thoughtfully. I was in awe. He had such a gift to be able to explain things to us in a way we could not only understand but completely grasp."

Bart Starr

QB, Green Bay Packers,
1961, 1962, 1965, 1966, 1967

Hank Stram

"Hank was an old-school kind of a guy. He was a very bright person. He was very funny and entertaining in the locker room and behind the scenes, but out on the field he was all business. Like most great coaches, he was an autocrat. There was only one way: Hank's way. He was tough, a real task master too. If you did something he didn't like, he would make you do it again and again and again until you got it right. He was also very strict when it came to the details. For instance, we had a certain coat-and-tie ensemble with the Chiefs insignia on it that we had to wear on road trips. Well, I remember one time one of the guys had a double-breasted suit made, instead of the single-breasted ones that everybody else had, and Hank fined him 500 bucks. That was a lot of dough in those days too, but he was insistent upon his players following the letter of the law. As an attorney now myself, I can certainly appreciate what he was after.

Kansas City Chiefs coach Hank Stram holds the championship trophy after the Chiefs defeated the Minnesota Vikings 23–7 in Super Bowl IV. (AP Images)

In fact, that's another thing I would say about Hank is that even though he was demanding, he was also a very compassionate person—especially if you were trying to better yourself off the field. For example, he allowed me to attend law school full time for three seasons while I was playing for him. How many coaches would do that in today's game? Sometimes I was late for a meeting or something because of a class obligation, and he was okay with that. If anybody else was late, he would read him the riot act, but not if you were a decent person and had his permission and blessing to be doing something to better yourself for life after football. That was big, really big, and not a lot of people know that about Hank.

I would also say that one of Hank's greatest attributes was the fact that he was color blind when it came to putting his roster together. Hank was one of the very best when it came to scouting, evaluating, and ultimately signing players from small black colleges. This is something we take for granted today, but it was unique in those days. Many of these guys were just outstanding athletes, but because of racial inequality back in the '60s, they just weren't scouted and given opportunities. So, Hank was ahead of his time in that regard. He went and signed guys like Jim Kearney and Otis Taylor, who were both out of Prairie View; and Buck Buchanan, who was from Grambling; and Emmitt Thomas, who came from tiny Bishop. Those guys were fantastic football players and really helped us to win the championship that season. Color was not an issue for Hank. Willie Lanier was the first black middle linebacker. Bobby Bell was an outstanding lineman, a future Hall of Famer. The list went on and on. Our talent, black and white, was just unbelievable. I was in awe just watching all the talent we had in practice day in and day out. It was amazing."

Bob Stein
LB, Chiefs, 1969

Hank Stram

"Hank was a great coach. He was very clever, very smart. He was so confident, just cocky about everything he did. He believed in himself and in his players. They were *his* players, and he stood behind them, no matter what. As a player, you knew that and you felt that. You just knew that he always had your back, that he would support you on game day, no matter what. He was a tremendous motivator too. Everything came back to attitude. He was always questioning us, challenging us about our attitudes. Attitude was what it was all about with Hank. He wanted us to have positive attitudes on and off the field, that was the key."

Jan Stenerud
K, Kansas City Chiefs, 1969

John Madden

"John was great, a really smart guy. He was a great motivator too. He was always going off on something or somebody, and he liked to pick fights. He liked conflict. He liked getting somebody to hate somebody else in order to get them fired up and pissed off. He would bring up something from the past, or whatever, to get guys upset—so that they would play mean and angry. It was a tactic. He was a master at that shit. He loved it, all the little mind games he would play. I will never forget his pregame speech, right before we were about to hit the field against the Vikings in the Super Bowl. It was very simple. We all gathered in and took a knee. He then said, 'Guys, this will be the biggest single experience of any of your lives…as long as you win. Let's go.' That was it. I was expecting a huge pep talk, like Knute Rockne or whatever, but that was it. He went with the old 'less is more' approach, and hey, you can't argue with the results."

Phil Villapiano
LB, Oakland Raiders, 1976

Chuck Noll

"Chuck was a great coach. What he was able to do was to take a program in the early '70s that had never really been a winner and had kind of been run down, and he transformed it. He instilled confidence into all of the players and got them to believe that they were good enough to be champions."

Mike Wagner
S, Pittsburgh Steelers,
1974, 1975, 1978, 1979

Bill Walsh

"The guy really was a genius. No kidding. He revolution-ized football as we know it and not just the Xs and Os part of it either. The way teams practice and train, the way they prepared, he was so ahead of his time. Football was much more of a smash mouth game prior to his arrival, and he changed a lot of that. He made it much more of a thinking-man's game. He was a great motivator and would use dif-ferent techniques for different people. He handled everybody in a unique way, a way that would get them to do their best. That was his gift, to find that unique way.

He was always thinking and trying to better himself. He valued the power of information too. I remember when I signed with the Niners, he invited me up to his office just a few days after I arrived in camp to have lunch with him. I was terrified. He knew that I had spent my rookie season the year before with Dallas, so he asked me all about [Cowboys head coach] Tom Landry. He wanted to know how he did things. He wanted to pick my brain and find out how other guys found success. Tom was obviously an icon in the coaching world, and Bill had a lot of respect for him and how he went about his business. Dallas was a

Steelers coach Chuck Noll (right) and quarterback Terry Bradshaw pose with the championship trophy following a welcome parade through downtown Pittsburgh on January 13, 1975. The Steelers defeated the Minnesota Vikings 16–6 in Super Bowl IX. (AP Images)

top-down organization, where everything went through Tom, whereas with the Niners, it was much more of a collaborative effort. Coaches and players interacted, had discussions, and then came up with game plans and strategies. Even though their two styles were like night and day, just polar opposites, he wanted to understand what made Tom tick—and he wanted to get the information from my point of view. He truly valued my opinion, and that meant a lot. What an insightful guy. He also had an unbelievable sense of humor, which a lot of people don't know about him. I think about Bill a lot, I really do.

Bill had a formula for winning, and it worked. He used to use a lot of analogies about mountain climbing. He would talk about how much work it took to get to the top of Mt. Everest. He talked about the base camp and then about how you had to get acclimated to the altitude in order to get to the first mountain camp. From there you had to get to your second mountain camp and on and on, until you eventually get a rare opportunity to get to the summit. He talked about how sometimes you do all that work and the weather gets bad and you have to turn around and head back down. Sometimes you get there, but other times you don't—that was his message. But you won't have a chance to even get there unless you put in the work and implement your plan. Bill always had a plan, and that was what made him so successful in my eyes. Bill and his staff got us to that last mountain camp, year in and year out, right there where you could see the summit. Sometimes we made it, while other times we came up short—for whatever the reason. That was the thing with the Niners in those days; we were always right there and always had a chance."

Mike Walter
LB, San Francisco 49ers,
1984, 1988, 1989

Blanton Collier

"Blanton was an underrated coach. I think he deserves to be in the Hall of Fame, I really do. While Paul Brown was probably the coach I learned the most from in my career, I would say that Blanton was the most knowledgeable football-wise. He had a level of brilliance when it came to understanding the nuances of the game. He wasn't dynamic like Brown was, he was more reserved, but he was just a very astute person. Great, great coach."

Paul Wiggin
DE, Cleveland Browns, 1964

Bill Parcells

"Coach Parcells was tough. He was always pushing us extremely hard, that was his style. I didn't understand it at the time because I was just a young guy when we won the Super Bowl, but after my 12th year in the league, I eventually got it. Yes, there was a method to his madness. Bill's philosophy was that you proved yourself on the field. Period. He was fair. You might not have liked what he said all the time, but he backed up his assessments with film—and the eye in the sky don't lie. We watched tons of video under him, and that was a really powerful tool. He wanted us to see what we were doing wrong so that we could fix it, and he wanted us to see what we were doing right so that we could keep doing it—or even do it better. He pushed you to a limit but never pushed you past it. He didn't want you to get injured or so tired that you couldn't do your job. He made sure we were very well prepared, because he certainly was. He did his homework and knew the game extremely well, maybe better than anybody in those days. Seriously. He had such a tremendous understanding of the game, and not just the offense and defense—he was a special teams guru as well, which a lot of people probably don't realize. It was amazing how he could break a game down. The guy was a genius at putting together game plans. He was so tactical and smart. That just kind of rubbed off on all of us over time. Overall, he was just a great coach—maybe one of the best ever."

Brian Williams
OL, New York Giants, 1990

CHAPTER
5

Champions for Life

Winning the championship is without question one of the most meaningful experiences of a player's life, both on and off the field. It will define him and ultimately change him forever. He will always be remembered as a champion after that, a title nobody can ever take away from him. The life lessons that are learned from that experience take years to sink in and be absorbed. For many of the players who had been out of the game for decades, the insight they had gained from those experiences was nothing short of remarkable. Most of them would go on to find success in the business world, in their lives after football, and I wanted them to share some of those takeaways that they felt were easily transferable into everyday life. So I wanted to leave you with some nuggets of wisdom and I hope you too can use these to find success and happiness in your own life.

WHAT LIFE LESSONS DID YOU LEARN FROM WINNING A CHAMPIONSHIP?

"There are two big things for me. The first is execution. I've been in commissioned sales since 1977, and in that line of work you get what you harvest. In order to harvest, however, you have to execute. The second thing is knowing your enemy, your competitor. You have to know them inside and out, understanding what they will and won't do, so that you can be mentally prepared when you get the opportunity to make the sale. All of that came from learning the game under Vince Lombardi. He demanded excellence from his players and just would not tolerate mistakes."

Donny Anderson
RB/P, Green Bay Packers, 1966, 1967

"There are a few things that stand out to me. Teamwork and dedication are the main things, but beyond that I think just the notion that nothing comes easy. If you work hard, practice hard, and stay dedicated to your goals, then success will always be attainable for you. That was how I played and how I ran my business after football. There's no secret. Great teamwork requires having great teammates, and I had some great teammates, many of whom I was fortunate enough to end up with as wonderful friends long after my playing days. These guys have been there for me throughout my entire adult life. What more could you ask for?"

Bobby Bell
DE, Kansas City Chiefs, 1969

"I was only in my midtwenties when I won those championships, and I didn't really know that much about life back then. All I was interested in was playing football. It wasn't until years later that I really realized what it all meant. I think the biggest thing for me that I took away from it all was the importance of the little things. In football, as well as in life, sometimes it's the little things that can mean the difference between winning and losing. Therefore, you should never underestimate the little things. To put this all into perspective, I believe the difference between us winning and losing that championship game in 1958 came down to us being able to execute one single play. It was definitely the turning point. We paid attention to a small detail that had come up at the most critical time, and luckily, due to our intense preparation, we were able to capitalize on it. We adjusted a play that was doomed in its original form, but we had a plan B all ready to go, an audible, that worked, and ultimately that critical adjustment probably gave us the win. That play kept our drive alive so that we could get down and kick a field goal to send it into overtime. So, being prepared and paying attention to the little things, those were the big takeaways for me. Without them, quite honestly, I don't think we would be having this conversation.

Another thing I would say is that there is great value in failure, if you can learn from your mistakes. For instance, one of the things I am most proud of in my career is the fact that I never fumbled the ball. Ever. I was charged with one, but the official blew the call. Seriously, I never had possession of it—so I don't count that one. Anyway, people often ask me about how I was able to always hold on to the ball, and I tell them that it all went back to my senior year at SMU. We were playing a key game against our big rival, Texas, and I had two big fumbles inside their 30-yard line that ultimately cost us the win. We wound up tying the game, 13–13, but then lost the Southwest Conference championship by a half game. So in my eyes those two fumbles cost us a trip to the Cotton Bowl, which was really hard to swallow. That so aggravated me; I was just beside myself. It left an indelible imprint on my brain, and I swore it would never happen again. Nobody had ever really talked to me at that point about how to carry the ball, how to put it away and protect it; it wasn't talked about a whole lot I suppose back in the early '50s. So, I worked my tail off every day in practice from there on out and learned how to protect the ball. I would catch upward of 100 balls a day, and every time I caught it I slapped it under my arm and into my rib cage with a tight grip. Over and over and over again I did this until it just became second nature. Thousands and thousands of times I did this, day after day, in practice and in games. It became an ingrained memory, a habit. That's what it takes to perfect something, practice and determination. I remembered how badly I felt when my teammates couldn't go to the Cotton Bowl and never forgot that."

Raymond Berry
WR, Baltimore Colts, 1958, 1959

"Passion, teamwork, and a belief that you can get it done—those are the three big things for me. First, you have to have a passion for what you do in life; that's the key to success in my eyes. Second, you have to be a good teammate. Working together alongside so many different people with different personalities, that's not always an easy thing. Teamwork is totally necessary though in order for your team to be successful. Lastly, you gotta believe. If you believe that you can do it, whether it's in sports, business, or life, that's when amazing things can happen. You have to believe. So, if you are able to put all of those things together, then the sky is the limit in my opinion."

Jerome Bettis
RB, Pittsburgh Steelers, 2005

Diamonds Are Forever

Following the 2003 Super Bowl win over Carolina, Patriots owner Bob Kraft bought the largest Super Bowl rings ever, 107.3 grams, with over five carats of diamonds. Here is reaction to those rings from some of the team's key players.[1]

"When I look at that ring, I think about minicamp, training camp, and all the tough battles we had to fight against some great opponents. There were games that no one thought we would pull out. Then, it all culminated in winning the Super Bowl. I still get chills whenever I watch the highlights from that game. I'm a very emotional person, and this ring makes me tear up when I think about everything it took to get it. It's the most beautiful ring I have ever seen, and more importantly it represents one of the most wonderful times of my life." — **Tom Brady,** Quarterback

"This ring symbolizes an amazing year. It's something most players spend their lifetimes trying to achieve, so to have the opportunity to be out there and do it, it's just an unbelievable feeling." — **Adam Vinatieri,** Kicker

"To me what this ring symbolizes is many things: undefeated at home, 15 victories in a row, two Super Bowls in the last three years—those are historic things. So when I look at that ring it reminds me that we are champions forever." — **Teddy Bruschi,** Linebacker

"You can't pay for something like this with money. It just takes hard work; blood, sweat, and tears; and a whole lot of sacrifices. This is why we do what we do." — **Richard Seymour,** Defensive End

"Just from the appearance alone, you know that you accomplished something major. I'm just very happy to be a part of this team, one of the best teams in the history of the NFL, and this ring signifies that." — **Ty Law,** Cornerback

"To me, you can never stop working on the details. As a kicker, I can tell you that every single little thing matters. Each kick is a process made up of a bunch of little things. As soon as you get too confident or start taking shortcuts, bad things are eventually going to happen. So, whether it's in football or life or wherever, you have to watch out for the little things."

Mason Crosby
K, Green Bay Packers, 2010

"The big takeaway for me is the power of the team concept. A great team is dependent on the capacity of its members to accept others who are different from them. Great teammates communicate with each other, they love each other, they support each other, and they perform with them—regardless of whether or not they agree with them or their politics or whether they have the same color skin. The great ones win in the final analysis because the men respect each other and love each other and will not let each other down. That's true in combat I'm told, and I'll guarantee you it's true with great football teams."

Bill Curry
C, Green Bay Packers, 1965, 1966;
Baltimore Colts, 1970

"I learned how to win, I learned how to motivate others, and I learned how to build a successful team around me. I learned all those things in football and was able to apply them to business."

Willie Davis
DE, Green Bay Packers,
1961, 1962, 1965, 1966, 1967

Packers kicker Mason Crosby (2) holds up a newspaper after the Packers'
31–25 win over Pittsburgh in Super Bowl XLV. (AP Images)

"I don't think you learn from winning, you learn from competing and from building something with a group of guys.
When you have a plan, you build it, execute it, and then see
it come to fruition and have success, that's what it's all about.
It's not just winning, it's the whole process. It's the lead-up to
it that really is fun. Working with the coaches, working with
the players, seeing positive results, the satisfaction of seeing
something that you designed working the way it was supposed to—it's all of that. Don't get me wrong, winning is the
ultimate prize in sports as well as in business, but you gotta
do it the right way and with the right people alongside you.

Mike Ditka is carried off the field by Steve McMichael, left, and William Perry after the Chicago Bears' 46–10 victory over the New England Patriots in Super Bowl XX. (AP Images)

You can't do it alone either. It takes a team of people who all buy into that same vision coming together in the end. When that all happens? That's when it gets exciting."

Mike Ditka

TE, Dallas Cowboys, 1971;
Head Coach, Chicago Bears, 1985

"You gotta be tough. Guys were a lot tougher in my day. If you were hurt, you just sucked it up and played, otherwise your backup was going to take your job as well as your paycheck. Nowadays to see the way these guys get hurt all the time, it's a joke. You see them get hit, and they lay on the ground for 15 friggin' minutes. The team trainer runs out there, the team doctor runs out there, then the team chaplain runs out there to read the guy his last rites—it's ridiculous! Then the guy jumps up and runs off the field, like

nothing happened. Unbelievable. These guys today aren't
very tough in my book, but hey, what the hell do I know?"

Art Donovan
DT, Baltimore Colts, 1958, 1959

"The best group of individuals doesn't always win it. Our
most talented teams actually didn't win it, but rather it was
the team that came together, that persevered, that fought
through adversity and stayed together. That's how you win
championships, when you get a group of individuals who
can put everything else aside and come together as a
team, all focused on accomplishing one common goal. It's
true in football, it's true in business, and it's true in life."

Tony Dungy
DB, Pittsburgh Steelers, 1978;
Head Coach, Indianapolis Colts, 2006

"For me it's the realization that sometimes character is more
important than talent. High-character guys help to build
chemistry, and chemistry wins football games. When I look
back at the 1985 Bears and the 2006 Colts, I see a very
important common denominator. Both teams had a lot of
high-character guys in key positions. Mike Singletary,
high-character guy. Walter Payton, high-character guy.
Peyton Manning, high-character guy. Jeff Saturday, high-
character guy. Gary Brackett, high-character guy. When you
get respected veteran leaders like that standing in front of
your team in the locker room and out on the field, influenc-
ing the younger guys, that's when you have success. So, you
need for your best players to be high-character guys, that's
so important. That right there, as I have learned over the
years, means a *whole* lot. With the right character people on

your team, even though you might not have the most talent, you've still got a good chance of being successful. So for me, as a head coach now, I too will be looking for high-character players to fill those leadership roles on my teams."

Leslie Frazier
CB, Chicago Bears, 1985;
Assistant Coach, Indianapolis Colts, 2006

"Teams win championships, not individuals. That was the big lesson for me that I took away from winning the Super Bowl. It's true in football, and it's true in business and in life."

Mike Garrett
RB, Kansas City Chiefs, 1969

"The biggest thing for me was simply to never quit. I learned that from Vince Lombardi. You just have to keep your shoulder to the wheel and keep on pushing. That's it. There's no magic formula for success other than hard work and a determination to never quit. As long as you can hang in there and keep after it, then anything is possible."

Forrest Gregg
OT, Green Bay Packers,
1961, 1962, 1965, 1966, 1967

"For me it was about being a professional and everything that entails. Playing at this level, it's not like high school and college where you could just be dominant because you were simply better than the guy across from you. At this level you have to really work at your game and on the little things. If you're a wide receiver and run a 4.3 [40-yard dash time] in college and can just blow by opposing cornerbacks, that all changes when you get to the pro level because that corner who's covering you now also runs a 4.3. So, you have to really work at your craft and constantly work on getting better. Because the reality is that if you don't work and get better, you're going to be out of a job. That's why you see so many talented players who excelled in college never make it in the NFL. It's those little things, the stuff that separates professionals from amateurs. The playing field is leveled immediately when you step up to play with the big boys, and if you can't cut it you're not going to last very long. It's the same in the business world that I am in today. You have to work on getting better and better each day and can never be complacent. You have to work hard, there's no secret. You're either getting better or you're getting worse—you don't stay the same in my opinion. You can't just sit back and think that you're gifted and that you can get it done. So, that was the big takeaway for me."

Jack Ham
LB, Pittsburgh Steelers,
1974, 1975, 1978, 1979

"You have to be able to minimize stress and anxiety. Sometimes you can be your own worst enemy. So, the secret is that if you believe you can accomplish something, then you will have a lot better chance of accomplishing it. Case in point: I remember when we were getting ready to play in the AFC Championship Game against Seattle. It was the first time I had ever advanced that far into the postseason, and I was really nervous. Our coach, Tom Flores, who I think was a mastermind when it came to pulling our team together and saying just the right things to help us stay unified, grounded and focused us on our task, talked to us before the game, and very nonchalantly said, 'Well men, it's just another game; I'll see you at the hotel tonight.' That attitude kept us relaxed. If our leader felt that way about it, then how could we feel stressed out? If he had come in and given us this big rah-rah speech about how we had worked hard all year and this was the biggest game of our lives, then we would have been much more stressed out and worried and probably not been able to perform as well. So, the big takeaway for me is to be able to eliminate the stress from situations like this by being relaxed and confident. If you can just focus on doing your job, and not all the other stuff, that's the key. Great players and great teams are able to do that, and do it consistently. They actually love those situations and thrive in them because they don't feel the stress. If you feel it [stress] you fail, that's the bottom line—in football as well as in life."

Mike Haynes
CB, Los Angeles Raiders, 1983

"It taught me to never take anything for granted. When I think about how many outstanding players don't have Super Bowl rings, it really makes me appreciate it that much more. You just never know in this game, you never know. So, when I think about all of those guys, it just makes me appreciate it that much more."

Ted Hendricks
LB, Baltimore Colts, 1970;
Oakland Raiders, 1976, 1980;
Los Angeles Raiders, 1983

"When I look back at my career, I think the thing that stands out the most is about what it takes to be a professional. When you become a professional, in anything, it's all about being the best of the best. And it's about winning. Winning is what it's all about. Sure, winning is important at the high school and collegiate levels, but it's not the end all, be all. Once you turn pro, however, it's all about winning. Big difference. This is your job, to win, and you get paid money to do so. Sometimes a whole lot of money, and the people paying you that money want to see a return on that investment. Winning is the name of the game at this level, that's just the bottom line. I'm proud to say that I was a winner. Those four championships will forever be a part of who I am and my legacy; they can never take that away from you."

Paul Hornung
HB, Green Bay Packers,
1961, 1962, 1965, 1966

"I would say not to give up, that you can always pull the good out of any situation. So many bad things happened to us that season, both on and off the field, but we hung in there and believed in ourselves. We never let injuries or other distractions get to us, and that was why we were able to win the championship."

Cullen Jenkins
DE, Green Bay Packers, 2010

"There were three big takeaways for me. First, to have success it had to be all about the team. Great individuals don't win championships, teams do. Second, everything worth accomplishing takes hard work. There's no simple way or magic potion or pill that you can take to get to the promised land without working hard. That's true in football and it's true in business. Third, as my dad used to always tell me, you have to be coachable. That means you have to humble yourself and not let your ego get in the way. You need to be a good listener and have to be willing to learn from the coaches as well as the veterans on the team."

Brent Jones
TE, San Francisco 49ers,
1988, 1989, 1994

"The big thing for me was the commitment to be the best you could be every single day. That has carried through in the business world for me today in the lumber industry. If you want to be successful, then you have to set reachable, attainable goals, and then work extremely hard to achieve them. The more success you want, the higher you need to set the bar and the harder you need to work. It's pretty basic stuff."

Lee Roy Jordan
LB, Dallas Cowboys, 1971

"I think I learned a lot about the value of hard work and about what it takes to make a buck. The Chicago Cardinals selected me out of Tulane back in 1950 and signed me for $6,500. It's not like we were making wheelbarrow loads of money in those days like they are today; some of my teammates were making $3,500 a season. I made the all-rookie team, and that entitled me to a $500 raise. I thought I had won the lottery. You couldn't live on that, so you had to work in the off-season to make ends meet. So I did whatever I could do. I unloaded freight cars, I worked on an oil rig, and I worked in a warehouse. None of us made that much, but we all loved to play football and were willing to do whatever it took to keep that dream alive I think. It wasn't an easy life, contrary to what many people think. We got by, and if you were smart you would walk away at the end of the season with a little extra money. I remember saving up to build a small addition on to my home one year, stuff like that. It was hard to raise a family on those wages though. It's crazy to think about how much the players today make. They make more just for showing up to off-season workouts than I made in 12 years playing in the NFL. Times have certainly changed, that's for sure. Those were marvelous times though, and I was proud to have won two world championships. I've got a whole bunch of wonderful memories and friendships too, and those have lasted a lifetime."

Don Joyce
DE, Baltimore Colts, 1958, 1959

"I learned a great deal from Coach Lombardi that I was able to apply to my life after football. He had a few key fundamentals he preached about often, things that were very important to him: commitment, consistency, discipline, perseverance, preparation, pride, and character. Pretty much anything you want to do in life, in order to succeed, requires you employing these characteristics. They're not unique to football by any stretch. I've used them often in my life and in business, and they all go back to what I learned from him all those years ago up in Green Bay. I've always tried to work hard and go the extra mile in order to be successful. If you do these things, it's no secret, you're going to have success sooner or later."

Jerry Kramer
G, Green Bay Packers,
1961, 1962, 1965, 1966, 1967

"The takeaways from winning it don't come right away; there's an aging process to it. I appreciate it now much more so than when it happened. I have grown so much as a person over that time and can now look back on the experience in a totally different light. People often ask me if I still do the 'toast' every year when the last undefeated team loses, meaning that our perfect season is still intact. The answer is yes, absolutely. Chicago had a shot in '85, Minnesota had a shot in '98, and New England made it all the way to the big game in 2006—but they all came up short. Indianapolis probably could have done it a few years back too, but they chose to rest their starters for the playoffs—which I think is a joke. I think that is just cheating the fans and the players. What a poor decision to do that. But that was what they chose to do. Anyway, our streak is still intact. It's fun, it really is, and it keeps us all connected from that team. Marv Fleming is kind of the ring leader of the 'cybertoast' these days, because we all still keep in touch via e-mail, which is something none of us could have ever imagined doing 40 years ago. Times have certainly changed, but thankfully that undefeated magical season has remained the same over all this time."

Jim Langer
C, Miami Dolphins, 1972, 1973

"When you get a bunch of people, regardless of their diverse backgrounds, working together on the same team—all with the same goals and aspirations—then anything is possible."

Willie Lanier
LB, Kansas City Chiefs, 1969

"The biggest takeaway for me was and still is 'Don't ever give up.' If I had a motto, that's what I would tell everybody in the world. Just don't quit, and eventually you will find success if you work hard enough. I look back to the year we won the Super Bowl, and the reason we won that year was because we refused to give up. Persistence, that was what it was all about. Even when guys were injured and beat down, we hung in there and stayed together. I remember we even had a bunch of older veterans on that team who had wanted to retire but stuck around another year in hopes of us finally being able to win it. Sure enough, thanks to their leadership we were able to get it done. They didn't want to quit on what we had started, and I am so thankful that they didn't."

Bob Lilly
DT, Dallas Cowboys, 1971

Discipline was the big takeaway for me. To be able to get 40 strong-willed guys to come together as a team, to live together and fight together for six months, you gotta have discipline. The coach has to be an honest person; he's got to be true to his standards; and he has to treat everybody the same. The players may not have to like the guy, but they have to respect him, or it won't work out. So, that was the big thing I learned from football that I was able to apply to business. I ran a very successful restaurant chain for many years, and the reason we were successful, without a doubt, is because we were disciplined in everything we did. I always tried to teach my employees like I was a football coach, with the same principles. My managers respected that and performed very well as a result.

Gino Marchetti
DE, Baltimore Colts, 1958, 1959

"For me it was the ability to always get up after getting knocked down. That was the challenge I always tried to overcome. Like being scared of your shadow or living in fear of failure. Life is always going to come at you with different obstacles. It's how you deal with those obstacles that determines how successful you are going to be."

Leonard Marshall
DE, New York Giants, 1986, 1990

"It takes a lot of hard work, but sometimes you gotta get a little bit lucky too. Things like injuries, which play a big part in games that are won and lost, you just never know about that stuff. We should have won it in '67, but I think we had somewhere between 13 and 16 guys who all had knee operations that season. It just about wiped us out. You gotta stay healthy, and sometimes that's out of your control. So, you just never know."

Don Maynard
WR, New York Jets, 1968

"Tolerance. When I came into the league back in the '50s there were racial problems going on. Racism was prevalent all over the country, everywhere. To be a black ballplayer in the NFL in those days, sometimes it was tough—both on and off the field. Off the field, you were 'limited.' There were restaurants where you couldn't eat. There were hotels where you couldn't stay. There were stores you couldn't go into. We couldn't go to the movies in order to relax before a big game. We couldn't even catch a cab if we wanted to go somewhere. We couldn't socialize with our teammates because if we went out together, we wouldn't get served. So, we were pretty much confined to one street in

*Jets receiver Don Maynard looks for a pass during Super Bowl XXX.
Maynard, playing on an injured hamstring, served as a decoy in the Jets'
16–7 upset win over the favored Baltimore Colts. (Herb Scharfman/
Sports Imagery/Getty Images)*

Baltimore, Pennsylvania Avenue. That was it. That was where all the black-owned cocktail lounges and restaurants were. If we wanted to go out for a nice meal or let off some steam, that was where we had to go.

Sadly, many of us were denied basic rights, not to mention opportunities, because of the color of our skin. I mean stuff like that was commonplace in those days. Those kinds of things injure your mentality and make you feel lesser than you should. I had some wonderful teammates who accepted me and treated me with respect though, guys like Raymond Berry. Raymond was a Christian, and that was the common bond that brought us together. I had many, many great teammates who were in my corner. I appreciate that and am proud to be friends with many of those fellows, even to this day.

On the field, meanwhile, you had unique challenges too. You know, football is a very mental game. You gotta know what you're doing, you gotta know how to do it, you gotta know when to do it, and you have to constantly be improving on all of those areas in order to become a top-notch ballplayer. So when things like racism came into your world, that really hurt. It bothers you mentally. There were many instances where opposing players called us terrible names. The 'N word' was very prevalent in those days, trust me. They did that purposely to get us off of our games. They wanted us to get mad, and frustrated, and maybe take a swing at them—so we would draw a penalty or turn the fans on us. So you had to be cool. You had to carry yourself in a certain way and act in a certain kind of manner that wasn't going to bring any extra attention to you.

I used to enjoy talking to Marion Motley, the late great Cleveland Brown. [In 1946, Motley became the second African American to re-integrate pro football, following

New York Giants safety Emlen Tunnell.] I used to ask him how he dealt with the racism. He then told me a story. He said, 'You know Lenny, I was told before a game one time that if I went into the end zone at any time during that game, that there would be a bullet waiting there for me.' He said that there were all sorts of terrible stories like that that he had heard from other players in those days. It was sad, it really was. Another person who really helped me was the late great Jackie Robinson, who was still playing then with the Dodgers when I first got into the league. He was the first black ballplayer, a true pioneer. The stories he told me were incredible. When he was with his teammates on the road, they would go out one door, and he would have to go out another. Things of that nature. The things he had to endure, it wasn't even human some of them. Yet, despite all of that, he still managed to be a professional and go about his business of playing baseball at an incredibly high level. He still maintained his dignity. Just think, had he not had all that extra tension and pressure, how good could he have really been? He never got to be the best that he could be because he always had to deal with all of that other stuff.

It's not right, but that's the way it was in those days. Players used to call him names, terrible names. They used to bring black cats into stadiums, and stuff like that, to taunt him and humiliate him. It was awful. The better he played, the harder they would try to get him frazzled. Yet, he was somehow able to overlook all of that and still play incredible baseball. He would step up to the plate and take care of business. He was one of the all-time greats, but just think how much better he could have been. It just ate away and took percentage points off over time. I had so much respect for Jackie because he had to go through all of it alone. He didn't have anybody out there with him to talk to. At least I had guys like

Lenny Moore carries the ball during the 1959 NFL Championship Game. Moore's 60-yard touchdown reception in the first quarter was the game's first score as the Colts defeated the New York Giants 31–16. (Robert Riger/Getty Images)

Jim Parker or Big Daddy Lipscomb or Jesse Thomas who I could lean on if I got down. I asked Jackie how he got through all of that, and he said, 'Lenny, many times I used to wonder myself how I did it.' Those were his exact words.

So I made it a point to talk to those guys, the Jackie Robinsons, the Jim Browns, and the Larry Dobys of the world, and ask them questions. Some guys were more outspoken than others and would say, 'Don't take it, man! Let them know what's what!' I didn't want to go that way though, that wasn't me. I didn't want to make trouble. I just wanted to play football and help my teammates win championships. The only thing we could do was to thank God that he had given us the talent, the ability, and the mentality to overcome all of that stuff. We just had to thank God. It was tough, believe me. Fortunately, I was able to be a part of two very special seasons with the Baltimore Colts in 1958 and 1959, and they can't ever take those away from us. Those are ours, we earned them."

Lenny Moore
RB, Baltimore Colts, 1958, 1959

"It takes a lot to be a champion. There are no excuses and no explanations, just answers and solutions. It's all about doing your job, doing whatever it is that you are supposed to take care of. It's about being a professional. It's about playing hurt. It's about always being a student of the game, always growing and learning to better yourself. It's about taking responsibility and owning up to your mistakes. When you do all of that, and everybody else does their job as well, then that's when incredible things can happen. The most important thing to me however, above all, is to put God first. I always do that, and that's why I am so successful both on and off the field."

Mewelde Moore
RB, Pittsburgh Steelers, 2008

"Everything in life, whether it's in sports or business, is always about working to get better. If you continue to get better, then everything takes care of itself. That's always been my theme in life. Get better as a person, get better as a coach, get better as a player, get better as a team—just get better. That's something you can control too, which is very empowering when you think about it. Everybody can work harder, study more, and do the little things necessary to improve. You just have to have that mindset that you are never going to be satisfied and that you are always going to try to get better. Beyond that, I think it's about people and relationships. Football is a game of people. As a coach, it's up to you to find out what your people can do. Once you know that, then you have to give them a chance to succeed and to be the very best that they can be. I would like to think that I, along with the rest of the offensive coaching staff, came up with a system that gave our players a chance to be the best that they could be."

Tom Moore

Offensive Coordinator,
Indianapolis Colts, 2006

"Winning the last game of the season is always the goal, that's why you play this game. It doesn't just happen though; it requires a whole bunch of preparation and hard work that starts months and months prior. Then you've got to be consistent. You've got to be able to play well consistently over an 18-week period, week in and week out. You've got to perform, even when you don't feel at your best—that's what it's all about. Everybody has talent at this level, otherwise they wouldn't even be out there. What separates the good from the great, however, is whether or not they have the will to get the job done. It's not just playing hurt either, it's extra workouts in the gym, extra time studying watching game film, and extra contributions to whatever else is going to help the team win. The good ones didn't worry about the individual statistics; they worried about the final statistics—those were the ones that mattered—whether you won or lost the game.

Beyond that, I learned a lot about life from being a backup for so many years. Look, in this game you have to accept your role for the betterment of the team. I was a backup for much of my career, but I made the best of it. I was able to play for 21 seasons in the NFL and am very proud of that. I played behind some of the great ones too—Johnny Unitas, Bob Griese—and I never complained. I just stayed mentally prepared, and when my number was called, I was ready to go. Sometimes it was tough, sure, because you wanted to get out there and contribute. I played in a lot of big games and wound up being a part of three Super Bowl–winning teams. I'm very proud of that. In life, you're not always going to be the starter, the star. You have to make the best of your situation though and do whatever you can to help your team win."

Earl Morrall
QB, Baltimore Colts, 1971;
Miami Dolphins, 1972, 1973

"Football is a team effort. Every man has got to do his job in order to make a play work and have success. It requires a lot of hard work too, and that's true for anything you do in life. You have to work hard, and you can't quit. You have to put everything you have into it; there's just no excuse for not giving it your all. I've run a very successful barbeque restaurant for over 30 years, and I can tell you that many of the life lessons I learned from football have applied to how I run my business. There's going to be good times and bad times along the way, but you just have to keep plugging away at it. If you believe in it, eventually it will work out, and you will have success. It's like the old saying goes, 'The harder you work, the luckier you get.'"

Andy Nelson
CB, Baltimore Colts, 1958, 1959

John Elway On Winning His First Super Bowl

"The low point was in 1990, when we lost our third Super Bowl in four years.... From 1990 to 1998, the years between Super Bowls, I got so tired of being asked the same question time and time again, 'Will your career be complete if you don't win a Super Bowl?' The media chose to focus on that perspective, and while I understood it, I just wanted to remove it.

The bottom line for me was that I *had* to be on a Super Bowl–winning team, that was my goal. My role in Super Bowl XXXII wasn't huge, but Green Bay's strength was in their secondary and their weakness was against the run—so if you've got a guy like [running back] Terrell Davis back there, then you've got to get him the ball. I had no problem with that. I knew that we were going to run the football going in and that my job was to pick up third downs. Whatever it took to get us over the hump, that was more than fine with me.

The big thing for me going into the game was for us to just be in it at the end. The three previous ones had all been blowouts, and I just wanted us to have a chance in the fourth quarter. I remember it being 24–24 with 3:45 to go, and when I was running out onto the field I was saying to myself, 'Boy, this is all I have asked for right here. This is my whole career right in front of me.' When Terrell scored that last touchdown, it was such a release. The weight off of my shoulders was unbelievable. The pressure was 10 times what I ever thought it would be.... To finally get that win, it made my career. You couldn't have written a better script.... When I was up on the guys' shoulders after the game, it was like I was born again. I could never have dreamed that a win could be so sweet." [2]

"The biggest thing for me was the team concept; everybody has to play together in order to have success. Everybody has a job to do, and they all have to be on the same page. One guy simply cannot carry the whole load; you have to be able to rely on each other. Beyond that, you need to have a common goal to strive for. Once everybody is dialed in on that, and they are all working together, then anything is possible."

Bob Nelson
DT, Oakland Raiders, 1980;
Los Angeles Raiders, 1983

"For me it was the realization that you can accomplish anything if you work hard enough at it. It also taught me about the importance of the team and about being a good teammate. I was a track guy and won individual track championships back in high school, but that stuff never even came close to measuring up to winning a team championship. Football is the ultimate team sport in that you can't have any success without your teammates all pulling their own weight. It truly takes a group of men who are all focused on accomplishing the same goal to be champions. There's just something so special about a group of guys all pulling together to accomplish a major goal like that."

Stacy Robinson
WR, New York Giants, 1986, 1990

"For me, failure is not an option. Somehow, some way, it's going to get done. Hard work, seven days a week, 18 hours a day. If that's what it takes, then that's what I'm willing to do today to make sure my business is successful. That's what I learned from winning the Super Bowl, that it takes a ton of extremely hard work and a determination of knowing that failure is simply not an option. There's not a lot of people who have that mentality, there really aren't. I mean a tough day at the office is nothing compared to a tough Sunday on the gridiron. To be able to deal with and persevere through the physical and emotional grind of an NFL season, it's insane. Most humans couldn't do it; what that entails, the sacrifice, and all the pain and suffering. It's crazy to put your body through all of that. For me, I played 16 years in the league and had to learn how to keep myself going. I had to eat right, I had to train right, I had to take care of my body 24/7 just to be able to get suited up each week. There were many Mondays where I couldn't physically get out of bed. So, to put your body through that kind of punishment week after week after week, you have to be determined. You have to wholeheartedly believe that failure is not an option. You know, a lot of people believe that football builds character. I actually believe that it reveals character. When you play the game at this level you find out pretty quickly just how deep you can dig. You find out how far you can take yourself on so many levels— mentally, physically, and emotionally. You figure out whether you have that ability to work with and trust that guy next to you or your coaches who have your back and want the best for you."

Bill Romanowski

LB, San Francisco 49ers, 1988, 1989;
Denver Broncos, 1997, 1998

"For me it's all about hard work. You work hard, you keep your nose to the grindstone, you overcome your difficulties, and then anything is possible. I had always had a hard work ethic, even as a kid, but certainly when you win a championship it reinforces the message, that's for sure. You know, I was a late bloomer. I was a second stringer in high school, I went to a small college, and I was drafted in the 16th round. They don't even have 16 rounds anymore! I worked hard though and eventually came into my own. I wasn't blessed with a lot of physical talents, but I made do with what I had, and fortunately I was able to play for the Colts for 13 seasons. Hard work, that's what it's all about."

Alex Sandusky
G, Baltimore Colts, 1958, 1959

"I think the big takeaway for me was balance. Don [Shula] had an extremely strong work ethic. He put in long hours and expected those around him to do the same. But he knew when enough was enough and understood that it was important to have a life outside of coaching as well. He knew that if you never spent any time with your wife and kids, then you weren't going to be very happy. So, what I learned from him was to make sure that the work you put in for preparation is commensurate with how much work is needed to be prepared. Other coaches such as George Allen and Blanton Collier, they both worked every night until midnight whether they needed to or not. I think that's unnecessary. It becomes a downer instead of an upper. Balance is the key. Sometimes you gotta work long hours and sometimes you don't."

Howard Schnellenberger
Assistant Coach, Miami Dolphins, 1972

"I learned that it takes tremendous leadership, passion, emotion, and love to win a championship. And it requires everybody being on board to get there. You have to dig down deep. You have to get into some stuff that quite frankly a lot of people aren't made of. Then, for anything great to happen, there has to be a vision for it, a catalyst to ignite it. From there you need buy-in, where guys commit to it and get behind it 100 percent. Once you win it, make sure that you enjoy the moment for what it is because there are so many different factors that go into being successful. To win a championship, you have to do everything right and then have some things go really well that you don't control. It's such a small margin for error. So enjoy it and savor it because it might not happen again right away."

Mike Singletary
LB, Chicago Bears, 1985

"There's no one man that can say he won the Super Bowl by himself—it takes a team. There were 11 of us on the field at the same time, and we all played together. Whether it's on the football field or in business, you can't do it all by yourself. You have to have a team of people around you who you believe in and trust, and they need to believe in and trust you too. It takes a team to have success."

Otis Sistrunk
DE, Oakland Raiders, 1976

"Winning it is great, but I actually learned a lot from losing the Super Bowl this past year [2011] as well. It's pretty humbling, that's for sure. It's so hard to have it all come down to the wire like that, losing the way we did to Green Bay. You have to look at the whole body of work, the entire season. The amount of effort and energy and time and sacrifice, it all goes into it. It goes all the way back to the off-season workouts. You play 20-some games, with preseason and postseason, not to mention training camp—it's a long journey. Then, you grind it out and persevere; you make it all the way through the playoffs and then get to the last game of the year. You work so hard, you put together a game plan, you execute it, and then you come up just short right at the very end. It's unbelievable when you think about it. It's so tough to come that close and still come up short. Somebody's gotta win and somebody's gotta lose though, that's football. Luckily, I've been on the winning side too, which makes me appreciate that so much more now that I have been on the losing side. I certainly don't ever want to be there again, I can promise you that. It's still a great accomplishment, to win your division and get to the Super Bowl. But being a champion and raising that Lombardi Trophy is what people remember. Look, successes and failures don't define you; it's how you react to them afterward that defines you. You have to keep it all in perspective. I learned a lot from losing it, and that's going to serve as my personal motivation to do whatever I can to help my team get back to the Super Bowl next season and hopefully win it. It's interesting, but the year we won it I have vivid memories of the celebration out on the field with my teammates and then with my family, kissing the trophy in the locker room, the victory parade, the ring ceremony, all the good stuff that's associated with winning. All I can remember from this past year when we lost it is losing. That's it. Again, winning? Much better than losing. Trust me."

Matt Spaeth
TE, Pittsburgh Steelers, 2008

"I think the greatest thing that I learned through all of that experience was the strength of two words that we have carried in our family forever: *attitude* and *love*. When I speak of the word *love* I am talking about closeness, companionship, compassion, understanding, and the togetherness of loving your teammates. Then you have attitude, which I think is the strongest word in our vocabulary. Attitude, in my opinion, determines your altitude, it truly does. When you can have that kind of attitude going for you, you are going to be very, very difficult to beat. What's unique about attitude is that you control it. You control how you are going to react, perform, and adjust under difficult conditions. It's all about attitude and love; if you have those two you can accomplish anything."

Bart Starr

QB, Green Bay Packers,
1961, 1962, 1965, 1966, 1967

"I think it all boils down to people and about the power of getting along. I think back to the makeup of that 1969 Chiefs team and what was going on in the world at that time. This was one year after Martin Luther King and Bobby Kennedy's assassinations. There were race riots, war protests—it was a tumultuous time in American history. On our team, however, it was like we were in a bubble. The leaders on our team, black and white, simply would not tolerate any negative energy. That was a big factor. Everybody got along. We didn't have any real jerks on the team; it was a bunch of really good guys. Many of us still stay in touch all these years later, which is wonderful. So the big takeaway for me with all of that is the power of getting along with teammates and coworkers, despite the fact that maybe you don't have that much in common with them. Hey, in football you could have a teammate who you wouldn't spit on if he was on fire, but you *have* to get along with him and have his back. That's just the nature of the game. If you don't, then your team is not going to be successful. Guys have to get along and be professional. So for us, to not only get along, but to genuinely like each other to boot—that was just gravy."

Bob Stein
LB, Kansas City Chiefs, 1969

"The biggest thing that I took away from winning the Super Bowl was the power of teamwork. My career now involves working with some of the world's top architects and engineers, and our success is all about the team concept. In order for us to have success, we have to work together. It's never about *I* or *me*, but rather about *we*. No one person can do it alone; it takes a group of individuals who are all committed and focused on a common goal. Once you have that, then anything is possible."

Jan Stenerud
K, Kansas City Chiefs, 1969

"For me it was all about working hard and always trying to get better. No matter how bad things are in life, you can always keep working and bettering yourself. If you do, and you believe in what you are striving for, then eventually good things will happen. I got to Green Bay in 1958, and we only won one game that season. It was the worst team in Packer history—and that's going back all the way to 1919. Two years later, in 1960, we made it all the way to the championship game, where we lost to the Philadelphia Eagles, and from there we won two straight world championships in 1961 and 1962 when we beat the Giants back to back. Who could have imagined that the worst team in the league in 1958 would be two-time champions just five years later? We went from the outhouse to the penthouse, which was a pretty gratifying thing to do."

Jim Taylor
RB, Green Bay Packers,
1961, 1962, 1965, 1966

"There were several big life lessons that I learned from winning the Super Bowl. For starters, I learned that hard work *does* pay off. I learned that playing together as a team *does* make a difference. I learned that it takes a team to have success and that the world *does not* revolve solely around any one individual. And I learned that when a group of people commit themselves to a singular purpose, amazing things can happen. I also learned a very valuable lesson from losing the Super Bowl as well. You see, after winning it in 1983, we got beat the following season by Los Angeles [Raiders] 38–9, which was just brutal. What I learned from that though is that you can't ever take anything for granted. Nothing is guaranteed. And furthermore, it can all be taken from you in an instant—which was what happened to me midway through the 1985 season when I suffered a career-ending injury. Nope. You just never know."

Joe Theismann
QB, Washington Redskins, 1982

"My big takeaway from winning it is that all things are possible. Don't ever think that you can set the bar too high because when you work hard enough, good things are going to happen. We set the bar from the first day of training camp to win the world championship, and we didn't waver from that goal throughout the season. We were focused on that goal as a team. Successful teams visualize success like that and are able to deliver in the end. I just feel very blessed to have been a part of such an amazing group of individuals who were all focused on that one goal. You've got to dream big, or big things will never happen. That philosophy, now that I am out of football, kind of bleeds over into everything I do. My identity has always been more than just being an athlete, so I am really looking forward to my career in life after football. I am pursuing a lot of my passions in life, including music and religion, and I know that anything is possible as long as I have a work ethic and a determination to succeed. I want to be the best husband and father I can be, and I know that the life lessons I learned from football will only help me to achieve that."

Ben Utecht
TE, Indianapolis Colts, 2006

"There were a couple big ones for me, starting with work ethic. Hard work was what it was all about for me. I don't think that there is anybody on this planet that can outwork me. I just made up my mind as a young kid that I wanted to be a pro football player, and nothing was going to prevent me from achieving that goal. I learned early on from my father and from my coaches all the way up the line that if you outwork everybody else then you're going to have success. It's the same in business too. The other big one is that you can't do it by yourself. You have to be a team player. You have to realize that it's not all about you, it's about the team. You have got to have teammates who are all focused on achieving the same goal and are all working together toward it. I had better seasons, personally, than the championship one of '76, but it happened for us that year because we all came together as a team. In order to have a great team, a great company, a great church, or great whatever, everybody has to carry their own weight, everybody has to work hard, everybody has to make sacrifices, and everybody has to come together. When that happens, and everybody comes together that way, that's when really special things can happen. That's when you can win championships."

Phil Villapiano
LB, Oakland Raiders, 1976

"You learn that nothing in life worth pursuing is easy. Hard work and effort are what it's all about, there's just no substitute. Now, that hard work doesn't always result in success, but it will usually result in gaining future opportunities. What you choose to do with those opportunities, however, is up to you."

Mike Wagner
S, Pittsburgh Steelers,
1974, 1975, 1978, 1979

"Hard work and preparation are the big things for me. I would like to say teamwork, because that would be the obvious answer here. But to be honest, I don't think you can really find the same thing in business as you can in professional sports. As much as you try to find that and as much as you try to say it's there, it's really not. Sports has this totally unique camaraderie all its own that you just can't find anywhere else. The time you spend with guys in the locker room, on the road, in practice, at training camp—it's where you build chemistry and trust in an environment that's unlike anything else. The sacrifice and pain you put yourself through in sports in order to help your teammates accomplish a goal is incredible. Businesses try very hard I'm sure to create that type of environment, but in reality I only think it exists in sports. That's what makes it so special."

Mike Walter
LB, San Francisco 49ers,
1984, 1988, 1989

"Teamwork was the big thing for me. The sense of knowing that you had all those guys looking after you is such a powerful thing. My business is football, so teamwork to me is what it's all about. I have been in this business all of my life, playing and coaching—it's all I know. And over all these years I can tell you that successful teams, both in sports as well as in business, always have people who believe in teamwork. It's the importance of being family, of being cohesive, and of caring about one another—that's what it's all about."

Paul Wiggin
DE, Cleveland Browns, 1964

"For me the big thing is to never take things for granted. The 1990–91 season was extremely difficult for me person-ally. I lost my father three days before training camp started that year, and as a result, I never got to share one of the greatest moments of my life with one of the most important people in my life. He was only 49 years old. We were very close, and he had always been there for me throughout my career, supporting me every step of the way. So, when he wasn't there for me that season, it was extremely difficult. What I learned from that situation was to never take things for granted. Now, I always try to be there for my kids, whether it's hockey or football or volleyball or whatever, I just really go out of my way to make time for them—no matter how busy I am. I appreciate every moment with them because I know how precious that time is. I recently sat through one of my daughter's U-12 hockey games, and all these parents were screaming and hollering and complaining about the refs. I just sat by myself, away from everybody else, and enjoyed watching my daughter out there having fun. I don't care; I'm just there for her unconditionally—win, lose, or draw. Life is too short to get caught up in all that other stuff."

Brian Williams
OL, New York Giants, 1990

"Accountability. That's the big thing for me. If you can breed that into a group of people, it's amazing what you can accomplish. If every lineman, every wide receiver, every equipment manager, every travel secretary, and everyone else on the team feels that if they do their job to the best of their ability, then the team will win—that's when you've got a really good shot at actually winning it. You need that buy-in from everybody, from top to bottom. It's rare, but when you can achieve that, it's pretty amazing. With the 49ers, we had accountability from the owner on down. There are certain elements that you have to have in order to be champions in this business, and the 49ers had them. You have to have the element of respect or love for each other that's built through breaking down cultural barriers that human beings have naturally. The organization has to be responsible to do that, to bring people together, and that was what Bill Walsh was able to do. They had created an almost quasi-religious affiliation between the team and the players. We called it the '49er Way' because we became affiliated with what it was to be a 49er. It was how we practiced, how we competed on Sundays, how we treated each other, how we prepared, everything that went into running a successful business. It got defined by us and brought out the best in us. It allowed us to self-propel to great heights. It all started with accountability though, because without it you have nothing."

Steve Young
QB, San Francisco 49ers,
1988, 1989, 1994

Jerry Rice On Fear of Failure

"If I have a single regret about my career, it's that I never took the time to enjoy it. I swear to God, this is true because I was always working. Right after the season, whether we won the Super Bowl or not, I would take two weeks off and go right back to training. The doubts, the struggles, that's who I am, and I wonder if I would have been as successful without them.

I was afraid to fail. The fear of failure is the engine that has driven me my entire life. The reason they never caught me from behind is because I ran scared. People always are surprised at how insecure I was."[3]

All-Time NFL Champions

2010 (Super Bowl XLV)—
Green Bay Packers

2009 (Super Bowl XLIV)—
New Orleans Saints

2008 (Super Bowl XLVIII)—
Pittsburgh Steelers

2007 (Super Bowl XLVII)—
New York Giants

2006 (Super Bowl XLVI)—
Indianapolis Colts

2005 (Super Bowl XLV)—
Pittsburgh Steelers

2004 (Super Bowl XXXIX)—
New England Patriots

2003 (Super Bowl XXXVIII)—
New England Patriots

2002 (Super Bowl XXXVII)—
Tampa Bay Buccaneers

2001 (Super Bowl XXXVI)—
New England Patriots

2000 (Super Bowl XXXV)—
Baltimore Ravens

1999 (Super Bowl XXXIV)—
St. Louis Rams

1998 (Super Bowl XXIII)—
Denver Broncos

1997 (Super Bowl XXXII)—
Denver Broncos

1996 (Super Bowl XXXI)—
Green Bay Packers

1995 (Super Bowl XXX)—
Dallas Cowboys

1994 (Super Bowl XXIX)—
San Francisco 49ers

1993 (Super Bowl XXVIII)—
Dallas Cowboys

1992 (Super Bowl XXVII)—
Dallas Cowboys

1991 (Super Bowl XXVI)—
Washington Redskins

1990 (Super Bowl XXV)—
New York Giants

1989 (Super Bowl XXIV)—
San Francisco 49ers

1988 (Super Bowl XXIII)—
San Francisco 49ers

1987 (Super Bowl XXII)—
Washington Redskins

1986 (Super Bowl XXI)—
New York Giants

1985 (Super Bowl XX)—
Chicago Bears

1984 (Super Bowl XIX)—
San Francisco 49ers

1983 (Super Bowl XVIII)—
Los Angeles Raiders

1982 (Super Bowl XVII)—
Washington Redskins

1981 (Super Bowl XVI)—
San Francisco 49ers

1980 (Super Bowl XV)—
Oakland Raiders

1979 (Super Bowl XIV)—
Pittsburgh Steelers

1978 (Super Bowl XIII)—
Pittsburgh Steelers

1977 (Super Bowl XII)—
Dallas Cowboys

1976 (Super Bowl XI)—
Oakland Raiders

1975 (Super Bowl X)—
Pittsburgh Steelers

1974 (Super Bowl IX)—
Pittsburgh Steelers

1973 (Super Bowl VIII)—
Miami Dolphins

1972 (Super Bowl VII)—
Miami Dolphins

1971 (Super Bowl VI)—
Dallas Cowboys

1970 (Super Bowl V)—
Baltimore Colts

1969 (Super Bowl IV)—
Kansas City Chiefs
(NFL: Minnesota Vikings)

1968 (Super Bowl III)—
New York Jets
(NFL: Baltimore Colts)

1967 (Super Bowl II)—
Green Bay Packers
(AFL: Oakland Raiders)

1966 (Super Bowl I)—
Green Bay Packers
(AFL: Kansas City Chiefs)

1965—AFL: Buffalo Bills; NFL:
Green Bay Packers

1964—AFL: Buffalo Bills; NFL:
Cleveland Browns

1963—AFL: San Diego
Chargers; NFL: Chicago Bears

1962—AFL: Dallas Texans;
NFL: Green Bay Packers

1961—AFL: Houston Oilers;
NFL: Green Bay Packers

1960—AFL: Houston Oilers;
NFL: Philadelphia Eagles

1959—Baltimore Colts

1958—Baltimore Colts

1957—Detroit Lions

1956—New York Giants

1955—Cleveland Browns

1954—Cleveland Browns

1953—Detroit Lions

1952—Detroit Lions

1951—Los Angeles Rams

1950—Cleveland Browns

1949—Philadelphia Eagles

1948—Philadelphia Eagles

1947—Chicago Cardinals

1946—Chicago Bears

1945—Cleveland Rams

1944—Green Bay Packers

1943—Chicago Bears

1942—Washington Redskins

1941—Chicago Bears

1940—Chicago Bears

1939—Green Bay Packers

1938—New York Giants

1937—Washington Redskins

1936—Green Bay Packers

1935—Detroit Lions

1934—New York Giants

1933—Chicago Bears

1932—Chicago Bears

1931—Green Bay Packers

1930—Green Bay Packers

1929—Green Bay Packers

1928—Providence Steam Roller

1927—New York Giants

1926—Frankford Yellow
Jackets

1925—Chicago Cardinals

1924—Cleveland Bulldogs

1923—Canton Bulldogs

1922—Canton Bulldogs

1921—Chicago Staleys*

1920—Akron Pros*

*Champion of American
Professional Football
Association, renamed as
National Football League in
1922

SOURCES

Chapter 1

1. Fox TV Show *Inside the Rings*, Feb. 6, 2011.
2. Super Bowl Post Game Quotes February 3, 2008. http://www.giantsgab.com/2008/02/03/super-bowl-post-game-quotes-tom-coughlin/
3. Interview NFL.com.
4. Greg Jennings interview with Rich Eisen on NFL Network *Game Day Final*.
5. Clay Matthews interview with Rich Eisen on NFL Network *Game Day Final*.

Chapter 2

1. Comcast *Countdown to Kickoff* with Jason Horowitz Interview, CBS.com
2. Interview with Ed Sabol, NFL Films

Chapter 3

1. Fox TV Show *Inside the Rings*, Feb. 6, 2011.
2. Jimmy Johnson 1993 Cowboys postgame locker room speech.
3. Fox TV Show *Inside the Rings*, Feb. 6, 2011.

4. Super Bowl Post Game Quotes February 3, 2008.
http://www.giantsgab.com/2008/02/03/super-bowl-post-game-quotes-tom-coughlin/

5. Fox TV Show *Inside the Rings*, Feb. 6, 2011.

6. Comcast *Countdown to Kickoff* with Jason Horowitz Interview CBS.com

Chapter 4

1. Fox TV Show *Inside the Rings*, Feb. 6, 2011.

2. "Sean Payton Sleeps with Lombardi Trophy: 'There's Nothing Like it,'" AOL Fanhouse, Feb 8, 2010.

3. *Bill Walsh: In Their Own Words*, NFL Films, 2000.

4. Press Conf. Transcript, Feb. 7, 2011.

5. Postgame Press Conference, Feb. 6, 2011.

6. *Jon Gruden: In Their Own Words*, NFL Films, 2003.

Chapter 5

1. NFL.com video

2. Interview. NFL.com

3. "Rice, Smith, LeBeau lead the Class of 2010 into Hall of Fame," *USA TODAY*, August, 8, 2010.